Training Soccer

Training Soccer

Barth/Zempel

Sports science research and consultant:
Prof. Berndt Barth (post-doctorate)

Meyer & Meyer Sport

The authors would like to thank Erich Rutemöller, coach and head trainer
of the German Soccer Federation, for his input and assistance.

Original title: Ich trainiere Fußball
Aachen: Meyer und Meyer, 2003
Translated by Susanne Evens, Sherey M. Gould, AAA Translation, St. Louis, Missouri, USA
www.AAATranslation.com

British Library Cataloguing in Publication Data
A catalogue for this book is available from the British Library

Training Soccer
Katrin Barth / Ullrich Zempel
– Oxford: Meyer und Meyer, (UK) Ltd., 2004
ISBN 1-84126-131-9

© 2004 by Meyer & Meyer Sport (UK) Ltd.
Aachen, Adelaide, Auckland, Budapest, Graz, Johannesburg,
Miami, Olten (CH), Oxford, Singapore, Toronto
Member of the World
Sports Publishers' Association
www.w-s-p-a.org

Printed and bound by:
FINIDR s. r. o., Český Těšín
ISBN 1-84126-131-9
E-Mail: verlag@m-m-sports.com
www.m-m-sports.com

....CONTENTS

Hi, it's me, Billy, the magic mouse! I bet you still remember me from your "Learning Soccer" book.

So now you are ready for some serious soccer training? Okay, I will come along again as your guide!

Caricatures of Billy you will find in this book:

When you see this particular caricature, Billy has a good tip for you. He will give you sound advice and draw your attention to mistakes.

This one indicates puzzles or questions. You can find the solutions and answers at the back of the book.

This figure shows you exercises which are also easy to do at home.

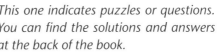

Places for you to jot down or fill out things to remember.

...................1 DEAR SOCCER PLAYER

Many kids are already soccer-crazy even as little toddlers. They only have to see a ball and the race is on to torpedo it into the goal, no matter what they might be using as a goal. You probably also started that way and maybe even practiced with our beginner's book, "Learning Soccer."

At first, kids can learn soccer alone. You just head out into your backyard or the school playground, an empty soccer field, against the garage door, really anywhere. It is not hard to find a meadow or vacant lot to use as a playing field. Unfortunately, today's kids can no longer play real street soccer, like kids used to play years ago. The streets are too dangerous now, neighbors are too protective of their flowerbeds and windows, and playground moms are too fearful about anything coming near their babies.

Once you have decided to learn even more about soccer, to train in the sport, and maybe even become a champion player yourself, then it is high time to join a soccer club. As a member of a club, you train under the guidance of coaches and assistants, who are generally very well-trained themselves, and who know how to teach all the intricacies of the game, especially to young people. They might have even been star players themselves in their heyday. In an organized club, together with friends and teammates, you will discover that you are playing better. You will get a lot of practice and you will also learn things by observation. You will have to see for yourself whether you feel comfortable in the team. Go to training on a trial basis for four weeks and then, together with your parents and the coach, decide whether you want to stick with it long-term.

But then give it your entire body and soul, your total zeal and passion!

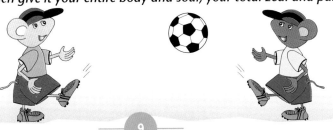

Let's start with a short story:

A strong athletic boy headed off into the mountains one day to climb a high peak. He cheerfully packed his backpack with food and drink and marched off full of vim and vigor. Since he did not know the way, it was tough going. He would climb upward and when he came to a point where he could not go any farther, he had to turn around and backtrack to where he could start over again. This extra going cost him a lot of his strength. If he was lucky, he would find a path that would take him a little higher up. After countless hit-and-miss attempts like these, he finally made it to the very top of the mountain, only to see that there were other people already up there. They told him that there was actually a good hiking trail to the summit. He could have taken it and would never have needed to go through all those detours.

Why did he not get a hold of a trail map? Why did he not ask somebody who had already climbed the mountain before?

Soccer training has a lot in common with our story of the "mountain climber". Many players have trained before you and some of them have even gone on to incredible success. You do not have to reinvent the game of soccer or how to train in the sport. You can simply learn from the experience of many who have gone before you. Think how much easier it will be! You can consider this book as your "trail map" - a compact tutorial on how to scale the "soccer summit" without coming up against a lot of detours. And, of course, you also have your soccer coach to help point out the right path.

It may happen that the opinions of experienced players, coaches and "book writers" will differ at times on the subject of training. This is normal. If you are not sure of something, ask various different people and make sure you fully understand why their opinions may differ.

But before you place this book under your pillow and go to sleep, thinking that now you will be sure to win in tomorrow's big match, there is still one important point we would like to make to you on your way to the top:

We are here to give you advice and to explain some great proven ways to train. But getting out there and doing the actual training – that is your job. Scaling the summit is something that is up to you alone.

All the training tips given in this book apply equally to girls as they do to boys. Sometimes, just for purposes of simplification, we may refer to "he" or "him", but players as well as coaches can, of course, be either male or female.

We hope you will have a lot of fun with this book. We know you will find a lot of interesting stuff in here that has the potential to get you up and running on your way to the "summit". And we wish you a lot of success along the way.

The Authors and Billy

This box should actually contain the names of five of Europe's most famous soccer clubs. But the letters somehow got all mixed up!

Can you figure them out anyway? What countries are these clubs from?

A	L	E	R		R	A	D	D	I	M

....

C	A		N	I	L	A	M

....

X	A	J	A		S	A	R	T	A	M	M	E	D

....

E	R	M	E	S	C	H	T	A	N		T	I	N	E	U	D

....

C	F		N	A	R	E	B	Y		H	M	C	U	N	I

....

.............................2 THE HISTORY
OF THE SOCCER MATCH

What is the object of soccer?
Two teams play against each other, each with the objective of defeating the other. To do so, the ball has to be hit with either the foot or the head into the opposing goal. The team scoring the most goals is the winner.

Who played soccer first?
Apparently the Chinese in ancient China, long before our time. The Aztecs of Central America also had organized games which were similar to what we now know as soccer. Soccer is even known to have been practiced by the ancient Greeks and Romans in Europe.

Why is England called the Birthplace of Soccer?
The actual inventors of today's soccer match were Englishmen. In medieval London, at the beginning of the 14th Century, two teams would fight for the ball using their hands as well as their feet. We even know that spectators would join in the play, or better said – the fray! And if the ball ever flew into water, the free-for-all simply continued on there, as if nothing was amiss!

For this reason, the government itself or individual city mayors would continually pass laws outlawing soccer (football). Finally in the 19th Century, in the English schools some rules were drawn up to do away with the rampant brutality of these, at times, very bloodthirsty games. It was decided in 1848, at Cambridge University that unlike the other very popular English sport of rugby, a soccer player could only touch the ball with his feet.

That is how the ground rules for today's, fair game were originally laid down.

The past 150 years in soccer history

1857 The first soccer club in history – *Sheffield F.C.* – is founded in Sheffield, England.

1863 The first national soccer association is founded in England, the first "regulation" soccer match in history is played in England: Harrow-School 3, Cambridge 1.

1872 First international match in the history of soccer: Scotland 0, England 0.

1873 The English sport of soccer makes the jump to Germany; Germany's first soccer club is founded in the city of Brunswick.

1874 The debut of the referee in England (whistles are not added until 1878).

1904 Founding of FIFA (Fédération Internationale de Football) (international Worldwide Soccer Association), organizer of the World Cup matches.

1930 First World Cup championship games are held in Uruguay.

1947 First live television broadcast of English soccer.

1954 Founding of the UEFA (European Soccer Association). Germany becomes World Champions for the first time in Switzerland.

2000 FIFA announces the award of the 2006 Soccer World Cup site.

2006 Soccer World Cup tournament to be held in Germany.

200_ ....

20_ _ ....

20_ _ ....

International Soccer

Which national teams do you think are the best in the world? Write down your top three!

Every four years, the FIFA organizes the **Soccer World Cup**.

Reigning World Champions

Men: _____

Women: _____

Meanwhile, the men's and women's **European Soccer Cup** also takes place every four years, offset by two years from the World Cup.

Reigning European champions

Men: _____

Women: _____

Youth national teams Players in different age groups. (For example, "U18" means that all players must be younger than 18 years at the beginning of the competition.)

The Champions League is the most important competition among European clubs.

The reigning Champions League winner is:

_____

TRAINING SOCCER

How young talent is developed

Taking the example of Germany for the moment, the DFB (National Soccer Federation) there has set up a talent scouting and development program, although many other countries around the world also have similar systems in place. The program in Germany gives top players from all over the country an additional once-a-week training session at a training camp (in addition to the training they do with their local organizations). Germany has more than 400 such training camps. This is one way to encourage up-and-coming soccer talent and offer young players more opportunities to develop their skills.

A career in soccer is thus within the reach of any determined and diligent player. Any boy or girl can apply and try for these training camps in Germany – and most likely you will find something very similar close to where you live, too!

Your coach will be happy to help you with this. You and your parents can also get in touch with your state or regional soccer association to find out more about the options available in your area.

So, how is your very first report card?

Great, Dad! My contract with the first grade has been extended another year!

...............3 Meet Michael Ballack!

Michael Ballack
born September 16, 1976 in Görlitz, Germany
6'2" / 176 lb.
Professional soccer player, Vice World Champion 2002,
Footballer of the Year 2002 and 2003 - Germany

Hi, Michael! You are a great soccer player! What is your secret?

There is no secret. All I can say is that I just love to play soccer. All my life, all I ever wanted was to become a great player, to play for a top team and to score a lot of goals. So I was always training very hard. Sometimes you just have to grit your teeth and keep plugging away, not get discouraged and give up simply because you have one bad day.

How did you first get into playing soccer?

Probably like all soccer players everywhere. I was outside playing with my friends every free minute I had. We would set up goals and then just play. My parents registered me in a club early on so that I could train correctly and play on a team.

What clubs have you played for?

I started with the BSG Motor Karl-Marx-Stadt, and then I was with the Chemnitzer FC until 1997, and then FC Kaiserslautern until 1999, and Bayer 04 Leverkusen up until 2002. I've been playing for FC Bayern Munich, Germany since 2002. I am also in the German national team.

What have been your greatest successes in soccer to date and do you still have more aims set for yourself?

When I was playing for FC Kaiserslautern, we won the German Champion-ships, and then in 2002, when I was with Bayer Leverkusen, we made it to the finals of the Champions League, and became the World Vice Cham-pions in the World Cup 2002 with the national team. But of course I still have lots of plans for the future. Each new national league season is like starting all over again. It is a brand new challenge each time. One of my biggest aims for the future is to become World Champion.

What does scoring a goal mean to you?

When you score a goal for your team, that is the biggest thing. But do not forget that we are eleven players fighting for this goal together, as one team. Everybody gives his all and whoever is in the best position goes for it.

That is why good preparation, winning one-on-one skills and precise passes are just as important. Soccer is not a one-man show – it is the team spirit that counts!

What does soccer mean to you?

As a professional, I earn my living by playing soccer. I was lucky to be able to make a job out of my favorite pastime. But I also know that no one plays soccer until retirement age and that injuries can make short work of any career. So I never neglected my studies and I graduated from school.

Do you still have time for other things besides soccer?

I take soccer and training very seriously. But it is also very important not to forget your friends and other hobbies you have. When I want to relax, I like to listen to music, go to the movies and get together with friends. But the most important thing in my life is my family.

What tips do you have for today's young kickers?

Soccer is a terrific sport. But you have to keep in mind that you will not get very far without dedication and discipline. You have got to go to training on a regular basis and make the effort. Get out there on the soccer or playground field as often as you can with your friends.
Have fun with sports and with soccer. Even if you do not become a professional player later on, you are still learning a lot of important things for your later life, things like camaraderie, teamwork, discipline, perseverance and stamina, plus order and organization. You will have many happy experiences, but you will also gain experience with defeat and failure. And that builds character.

Thanks for talking with us and keep up the great work!

Fan page

Favorite player: _____
Club/Team: _____
Position: _____
Highlights/Records: _____

Space for collecting autographs or pasting pictures

.....................................4 TRAINING –
THE RIGHT PATH TO SUCCESS

To play like your heroes, now wouldn't that be the tops! You want to be an ace in the penalty area, score amazing goals, gloriously steal the ball and be strong in defense. You have probably already realized during training and games that things do not always turn out the way you had planned or hoped they would. Besides, your opponents are also good players, maybe even better than you!

That is not a problem, because whatever they can do, you can do, too! But how can you accomplish all that, how can you become a really good soccer player – maybe even going all the way to the big leagues? Well, that is why we wrote this book, to help you train successfully!

Erich Rutemöller – the Head Coach from the German Soccer Federation training with youths

The path to the soccer summit

This book can never replace your coach. It will, however, explain why your coach is focused on training with you on your technique and your fitness, why he or she keeps harping on to you to improve your stamina, your strength and your speed, not to mention your mobility and maneuverability.

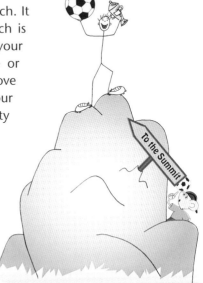

You will grow to understand why besides playing in actual games, it is necessary to perform and practice other exercises which at first may seem like they have nothing to do with the game of soccer at all.

You will learn how important pre-training or pre-game stretching and warming up can be. You will learn why you sometimes think you will never get any better and why you are not as good on different days.

You will also learn what you can do yourself during and apart from training to improve your performance and independently monitor and assess your own progress. That is precisely what the world's best soccer players do. After many years of training and countless matches, they know exactly whether they are in top form or not on any given day, and what they have to concentrate on in training in order to play a better game.

While you can consider your coach as a good friend and mentor, there are also times when he or she needs to be strict. And that is usually those times when that tempting little voice inside your head starts whining, "Come on, this is far too exhausting. Let's just call it a day!"

Active and concerted training

Training for the game of soccer encompasses all those things you need to actively and concertedly do in order to be able to play the game better.

 Active means that you are the one who has to train. You will not get any better by watching your coach running, scoring or jumping. Nor by putting soccer books under your pillow at night. Only by getting out there and training yourself; i.e. being active.

 Concerted means that you understand the sense and the purpose of the drills your coach gives you to do and that you can perform them independently. You might even think up your own exercises as well.

The opposite of an athlete's concerted training is the instinctive training of racehorses or greyhounds. They are only blindly following the orders of their trainers, which is the most they can ever do!

In your training, you are not just a docile follower of what you have been told. The difference is that you also understand why you are doing it. And that will ultimately pay off in your success.

By the way, this concept does not apply just to sports either; it will also serve you well in school!

Since a soccer player has to train for many years in order to achieve top performance, it makes sense to know right from the start what proper training really means and to learn how to do it. This will allow you to make greater progress in your training than other kids will in the same time, and you will end up being more successful. Besides, training will be a lot more fun!

Training has to be learned!

Proper training – but how?

Before you can benefit from concerted training, you have to ask yourself three questions:

What do I want to accomplish
What are the aims of my training
How can I train for them

What do I want to accomplish?
What are the aims of my training?

Active and concerted training calls for clear objectives. If you do not have an aim, training will quickly stop being any fun. You will not know why you are pushing yourself. Of course, the most important aim a soccer player could ever have, is to have fun playing soccer. You will only be able to have true fun in the long run when you have mastered a perfect technique, when you are faster and can draw on more staying power and, of course, score lots of goals. You are serving your team and your team can then win its matches. Or maybe you would rather just lose all the time?

At first, you probably set your sights on a big aim. You watched the World Cup or another similar exciting tournament on television. The team showers bear hugs on their scorers, the fans in the stadium go wild, the masses huddled around television sets rejoice with unbridled enthusiasm. And you think, "I'd like that!" And that is good!

But you do have to keep in mind that simply dreaming of victory will not make it a reality. There is a lot of sweat behind a celebrating champion and you will also have to accept many defeats along the way.

Besides your ultimate objectives, which are still far off in the future, you also have to set more immediate aims. For example, you set your sights on finally winning a one-on-one showdown against Tom, scoring a goal from farther away than ever before, or making it through the second half without getting totally worn-out.

Aims are what drive every ambitious athlete!

It is fun to achieve an aim you set for yourself and those times when it does not pan out, it acts as an incentive to spur you on. But do not set any impossible aims for yourself, only those which are realistic and which you can achieve in the near future.

Is not the coach the one to set the aims?

Maybe you are thinking right now that is what the coach is supposed to do. Is not he the one to tell you what you can and should achieve? Yes, and he will. He is also setting his own aims for training his players and he is drawing up plans he will use in helping you train. There are quite a lot of books and training programs for coaches as well.

But in the end, you as a player are the one who knows yourself best, including your own strengths and weaknesses. So you are also the one to best know which aims to set. And it is always better when you set your own aims yourself instead of having them "foisted" upon you by someone else. Then they are your very own aims and you are far more ready and willing to give your all in achieving them.

If you can tell your coach exactly what is holding you back and what you would really like to work on and improve at any given moment, then he will be able to follow up on it and give you much better support during training.

Imagine these situations coming up during training.
How would you react?

Your coach wants you to chip a high ball into the net with your instep from a distance of 50 feet. But you do not make it. Your ball never gets up into a trajectory; it just rolls flat over the grass.

The coach asks you to juggle the ball at least ten times. You cannot help but grin. What a piece of cake! Your personal record so far is 22.

Of course, coaches and athletes will sometimes have different opinions. Sometimes the aims you have set for yourself do not match those your coach has in mind for you. Keep in mind that a coach does not have an easy time of it. If you think the aims he is setting for you are too high, then he believes you are capable of more. If you think his aims are too low, then show him what you have really got!

Use the table on Page 28 to write down your aims. Include today's date. Use the second column to record by when you want to achieve this aim. Once you actually do achieve it, check it off and add the date you did it.

When the table is full, draw a new one and tape or paste it right here over the old one. Or you could also make your own "Aim Journal" to use for a long time to come.

What I want to achieve / Date	Date to reach my aim / Date I actually reached it
Score a goal in a match / June 22	*July / July 24* ✔
Juggle 20 times in a row	

Ultimate aim versus sub-aims

Example:
Paul played very poorly in the last game; the coach even had to replace him. But Paul also knows what the problem was. Because of his poor technique, all the balls were getting away from him! He decides he definitely has to use his training times before the next game to work on improving his ball control when dribbling. That is his ultimate aim. Of course, he will not be able to improve the whole of his technique right at the very next training session. This is why he also sets sub-aims for himself, to carry him along the way to his ultimate aim.

Here's how it works:

guiding the ball over a longer distance close to the foot   quick passes   zigzag dribbling   dribbling around opponents

poor dribbling technique   improved ball control

Or let's say that your headers are a little weak. You cannot expect immediate improvement here either. Some sub-aims to improve your headers might be:

 working on the strength of your jumps to make them higher and faster

 juggling the ball with your head

 more accuracy in hitting the ball with your forehead

By setting sub-aims for yourself with all the techniques described in this book, you will feel great when you achieve them, even if they might not yet work so well during an actual game. To improve your speed, sub-aims focused on sprinting times is a big help. To improve your stamina, focus on endurance times, and for increasing your jumping strength, make the height of your jumps into sub-aims.

Why do I want to train in soccer?
What is the reason for training?
What are the motives behind it?

The reason, sometimes called the *motive*, for training becomes the „mental engine" which drives it. It is what decides whether you go to training today or not. Whether you fight back or just give up in the face of failure or disappointment.

It is no problem to go to training when the weather is great or when you are bored. You meet your friends and teammates there, and maybe your coach even, means you have something really fun and exciting planned. But what about when your friends from school want you to go with them to the ice cream store, or there is something great on television when the weather is icky? Do you pack up your gym bag just as quickly then, too?

But if there is an intermediate aim that you want to achieve, no matter what, and you know that the next training session is extremely important as far as the team lineup, then it is not so hard to make your decision.

Figure out exactly why you play soccer and why you push yourself during training. Decide whether a certain motive is very important for you, somewhat important or of less importance.

Make the checkmark in each the appropriate column of the following list.

If you have other motives, write them down in the blank lines. You can also update this guide after a year or so. Your motives may have changed by then.

I go to training and strive to give my best performance

	very important reason	important reason	not so important
because I want to play as good as my idol.	☐	☐	☐
because I want to be more healthy and fit.	☐	☐	☐
because I want training to make me stronger.	☐	☐	☐
because I want to please my parents.	☐	☐	☐
because my best friend is doing it.	☐	☐	☐
because I do not want to disappoint my coach.	☐	☐	☐
because I will gain acceptance.	☐	☐	☐
because I do not have anything better to do.	☐	☐	☐
because I want to help my team win.	☐	☐	☐
because I want to see my picture in the paper.	☐	☐	☐
because I want to play for the national team some day.	☐	☐	☐
because I want to earn a lot of money playing as a pro some day.	☐	☐	☐
because I want to build character.	☐	☐	☐
because soccer is a great sport.	☐	☐	☐
because _____	☐	☐	☐
because _____	☐	☐	☐

The coach says to Max, "Run the 50-yard dash as fast as you can!" Max does his best and is completely satisfied with his performance.

Ollie is up next. The coach clocks a faster time for him. This really bugs Max even though just a few minutes earlier, he was quite satisfied with his time. He now wants to run a head-to-head race with Ollie; Max does not take this defeat lightly.

It actually does not matter what the final outcome is, because you can easily imagine that Max will definitely run faster the second time around. The direct competition with Ollie has motivated him to run even faster.

A very important reason for going the extra mile in training is that you know exactly why you are doing each individual exercise and why doing each of them will improve your performance.

If you are into it, you will get it!

How can I train so that I will achieve my aims?
How does training improve my performance?

Experts refer to pushing yourself in training as *exertion*. Just as each player is different from everyone else, his or her resiliency and the level of exertion he or she has to bring to bear are also different. When an athlete is not making any effort during training, he won't improve his performance, whatever he tries. But when an athlete exerts him- or herself too much, this can lead to exhaustion and to injuries.

Unfortunately, there is no precise chart for a player or coach to consult to find out how much exertion can and should be applied. Each athlete has to help out in this regard. Over time you will learn how to "listen" to what your body is telling you and to recognize when your level of exertion is high enough.

Applying the right level of exertion when training results in increased performance, because our whole organism adapts itself to the new conditions. Your heart expands, growing more powerful, and your muscles harden and become stronger. After some time of established regular training, you realize that those exercises which before used to leave you huffing and puffing do not even faze you anymore. If you were completely exhausted after just a 15-minute run before, it is now no problem for you to keep up the pace for at least 30 minutes, or even longer.

This then becomes the time to increase your exertion. Your organism will again have to adapt itself, and this is how we go about gradually increasing our performance.

Over the years, many sports scientists and doctors have studied and researched which soccer training methods are the best in order to return the best athletic performances and keep the body healthy and fit. Just rashly adopting any old course of training will usually not bring on the success you are looking for. It can even be harmful.

You have probably already experienced how, if you have not trained for a while, your performance the next time around is a little worse. In the first training session after your break, the exercises seem harder and your performance is no longer as good. You had to start again at a lower level of exertion than where you were when you wrapped up your previous training session.

Regular training beats irregular – hands down!

Do you still remember our example about the summit you want to scale? Laziness and irregularity in training retard the development of your progress and performance. You stumble backward on your path to success. It is as if you are taking two steps forward, but then one step back.

But often, it is not possible to train as diligently as you may have resolved to do. There are times when your schoolwork requires more of your attention, you go on vacation with your parents, your team does not get much time on the field, or maybe even your coach is short on time.

Yet those who have set athletic aims for themselves, do need to train two to three times a week. If you are 14 years old or older, you should be out there training three to four times a week.

If your training comes to a halt due to illness or injury, then of course you have to put your health first and concentrate on getting well again. But if you are not able to attend training due to vacation, a school event or any other similar reason, then at least try to stay in condition. Go jogging, do some strengthening or ball exercises in your room, or train your swiftness and maneuvering skills. You will find special exercises at different spots throughout this book. They will help make it easier for you to get back into the swing of things after you have been away from it for a while.

Before you read the next few pages, answer the following questions:

What makes a good soccer player?

What does a top-notch soccer player have to be able to do?

On what does his performance depend?

What makes a good soccer player?

We bet you came up with some good answers to the questions we posed on Page 36.

Our overview below depicts all the factors which can affect a soccer player's performance and the various basics which need to be trained. The reason the circles overlap is that it is impossible to consider these individual factors separately from one another. Everything is set within the circle of mental abilities since your mental state has a direct effect on everything you do. Important external influences also play a part.

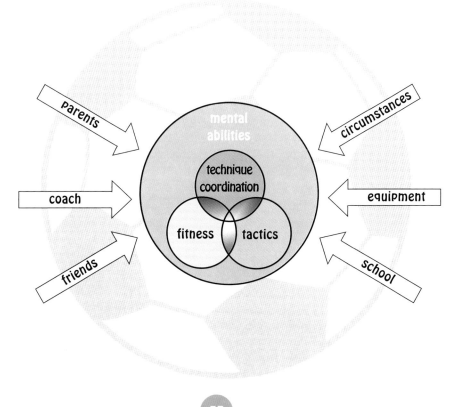

Soccer players who are fast and who have superb stamina and strength are referred to as being fit, being in good condition. Depending on the age of the players, a soccer match lasts anywhere from 50 to 90 minutes. It is therefore quite important to be fit enough to last the whole game.

Technique refers to those actions specific to soccer. This includes all the different types of kicks, gaining control of the ball and running with it, defense tactics, passing, dribbling and feinting.

So that all the movements of your legs, arms and your body as a whole which soccer requires will work in perfect combination with one another, you need coordination. You need to be able to do everything that comes up during a game in your sleep. When you are on the field, you should be concentrating on how the match is going, on your opponents and on the ball. That is definitely not the time to be pondering on the correct execution of a technique.

Tactics refer to the strategy you will use to defeat your opponents. Alone and in concert with your teammates, you defend your possession of the ball and thus your possible victory.

Your psyche dictates how confident of victory you are, how prepared or apprehensive you are for the contest, whether a bungled one-on-one or a ball kicked out of bounds will discourage you or spur you on to pull out all the stops instead.

Our illustration shows you other vital pillars in your life such as your **parents, coach, friends, training circumstances, equipment and school** (you can certainly list even more). These are all external things which have an influence on you and which will also affect your athletic performance. It is very important whether your parents are supportive or critical of your training, how good you get along with your coach, and whether you truly enjoy being together with your teammates.

When there are problems at school or stress within your family, you can not keep a clear head. It really does make a big difference whether there is a lot of cheering spectators out there, whether the sun is shining or if you like your new jersey, or whether you get booed, the grass is muddy and your old shoes are pinching your feet.

All factors combined add up to success!

You will only become a fantastic marathon runner if you are in peak condition, a wizard with a ball if you have a refined technique, or a world-class chess master if you have excellent tactics. But a soccer player needs all of that – and all at the same time! And when our psyche, our very control system, fails us, then everything can get messed up. It is just like having a powerful computer, but no software for it. Yet getting all the components set up in flawless working order all at once is a very difficult undertaking. That is why each component is trained a little at a time, step by step, in order to become a great soccer player.

What does all that mean for your own training?

The best training for young soccer players is to play, play, play!

During a game you have to run, kick, keep your opponents guessing, and have nerves of steel. That is what is the most fun and you can practice everything all at the same time. But maybe you have noticed that certain weaknesses always seem to crop up and you do not see yourself getting any better. All that is needed is some additional targeted training! If you feel exhausted after just a few minutes of play, do some extra jogging. If you are continually left behind by opponents, you have got to concentrate more on your sprints. When your attempts at passing or scoring could stand some improvement, it is time to pay extra attention to your shooting technique.

We have devoted the next chapter to explaining the individual factors in greater detail and discussing training methods. We will show you various exercises and drills you can do at home as well as how you can monitor and assess your own performance and progress.

5 TECHNIQUES

What is meant by techniques

The most important „tools" that man has are his hands. They allow us to do the most precise kinds of work. And yet except for the goalkeeper or for the throw-in, soccer prohibits their use entirely!

Remember your very first attempts at soccer? How virtually impossible it was to kick the ball in the right direction or at the right height, to stop it with your foot, or to pass it over to a teammate without losing it? Things only started to look up after much trial and error and frequent play.

There are soccer players who are true artists with the ball. They can juggle it any and all ways and amaze their fans with extraordinary tricks. They have a very good feel for the ball. This is an important prerequisite to being a top player.

Yet controlling on the ball is far more and also a bit different than just juggling. You want to score goals while preventing your opponent from getting any! To do that, you need to shoot, pass, dribble, and... so much more!

Players who want to excel at soccer have to learn and master soccer techniques. These are the basic tools of the soccer player.

You will be continually practicing techniques and sequences of movements in many different ways during your training sessions. You'll have to do it until you no longer have to think about each and every individual step it entails. Just imagine if you always needed to contemplate each separate motion within a full sequence before you could perform the whole thing!

For example, hitting a header:
"Note approach of ball – stiffen neck – coil body – eyes open – leap up at just the right moment – connect with forehead – quickly thrust upper body forward!"

You do not have time for all that during a match! You have got to concentrate on your opponent, the pace and the progress of the game.

Your movements have to become completely automatic!

Soccer techniques

By *soccer techniques* we mean all those special movements which are used during a soccer game played according to the rules. This includes executing all the different kinds of kicks, gaining control of the ball and running with it, passing it, the throw-in, etc. You have already learned the most important techniques during your first few years of playing the game. Your continued training now simply builds upon, refines and varies them, and adds some new ones in for good measure.

During actual play, the movements are executed quickly and confidently. You can barely even break down the sequence. But you will know from its success or failure whether everything was performed correctly or not. When a teammate and not an opponent gets the pass, when you maintain possession of the ball while dribbling and, of course, when the ball lands smack dab in the net (provided it is not your own!).

Of course you will not wake up one fine morning with everything suddenly and miraculously having fallen into place. You will be learning bits and pieces over the course of many training sessions and matches.

Learning the techniques

Being introduced to a new technique is usually accompanied by the relevant explanation from your coach. He will explain the entire sequence of movement, tell you what you should pay special attention to, and what mistakes you should avoid. Then he will demonstrate the technique for you.

Learning is a step-by-step process

You have certainly already realized that you rarely "get" things right the first time. You do not start out being able to perform them like a pro. After all, we are not magicians! If you want to learn something new, you take it step-by-step, a little at a time, and go from the easy to the difficult. Once you can do some individual movements well and you have practiced them long enough, then you are ready to take the next step. But avoid getting stuck in the "slow motion" rut, because when you are in the middle of a game, you certainly do not have that much time. Besides, when the ball is travelling too slowly, it does not have enough momentum. Once you know exactly how a movement sequence goes, then start practicing it at a fast clip.

Perseverance equals success

After you have been shown something and your coach has explained it to you, it is time to practice. Of course it is fun learning a new technique and trying it out. Your movements are usually very hesitant and imprecise at first, but you will soon notice progress. Your movements become continually faster and more confident and this will not escape the attention of your coach either. He is certain to praise you and that is a very strong incentive for you to practice even more and become even faster and more skilled.

Yet your coach can not be watching everyone all at the same time, so help your teammates out, just as they should be helping you. One athlete runs through the maneuver and the other watches him closely and tells him what still needs work.

And then, slowly but surely, the drills start to get boring. You do not sense any clear-cut improvement in your performance and the excitement of it being new is also gone. You start to think that since you have got this new technique down pat, why do you actually need to keep on practicing it? Or, you get to the point where you just might not feel like it anymore. But if you stop now, you will forget some of it again, and all that training will have been for nothing. Think about what you have resolved to do and overpower that "inner voice".

The path to increased performance

Right on the heels of rapid progress, you can have seemingly endless days of training, where you get the feeling that nothing is happening. This is normal. Just as there are always phases of rapid progress, there are also always stages of tedious drudgery on the long path to perfect technique. When you start thinking that something cannot get any better or faster, that you have already reached your upper limit and trying to go any higher would be stupid or pointless, keep on plugging away anyway. You will find that you will, in fact, go higher.

The movement is now automatic.

Apparent standstill: "reprogramming"

Conscious control of movement with a new technique. Concentration on every individual motion within the whole. Ongoing improvement in performance.

When you are in that apparent standstill mode, your body is preparing for the next stage of development in your performance. You could say it is internally "reprogramming" itself for the next level. Sometimes that seems to happen almost overnight. The key here is: Persevere! By the way, your coach knows this as well. Have no fear – he will let you keep on practicing diligently!

Some techniques you will learn relatively quickly. Others will take countless training sessions, even years.

Coordination

We need good coordination in many areas of our lives. Think about eating with a knife and fork, writing, painting, model building, also riding a bicycle, balancing on a narrow beam or swimming. Good coordination calls for total control of your body. Physical fitness experts refer to this as controlling – or *coordinating* – your muscles.

Here's how it works:
Your sense organs (eyes, ears, etc.) identify the immediate circumstances of the game and forward this information to the brain. Your brain then sends commands out to your muscles about how they should react.

Soccer calls for the absolute mastery of many techniques, which you will then use to complete a good pass, aim a deadly goal, or successfully monopolize the ball in a one-on-one contest.

Consider all that is going on when shooting for a goal, for example:
The ball is lying there right in front of you. Your brain flashes the order to your leg muscles: Kick! This command is as fast as lightning, seconds would be far too long. It all happens much faster than that. It goes along the network of nerves down to your legs. The muscles all work in coordinated concert with each other because our legs have many different groups of muscles working in combination (hips, thighs, lower leg, and feet).

The end result of this concerted *(coordinated)* interaction is kicking a goal:
run-up – draw back – pre-swing momentum – stiffening the foot – taking aim at the ball – connecting with the ball – kicking –follow-through of kicking leg

All of these are purely single and partial movements. But in their totality, they are recognizable as a kick. The better the coordination of each individual part, the more precise and sharper the kick. Our legs work like a *motor* being driven by the *brain*.

Game situations which require good coordination

Quick actions in tight spaces under attack from an opponent

For example: You are the center forward and you have the ball. You have your back to the net. An opponent is breathing down your neck behind you. You want to get round him and have a shot at goal.

Evading an opponent's attack

For example: An opponent comes rushing toward you wanting to steal the ball away and you make a skillful feint to get him on the "wrong" side.

Skillful ball control in the face of an opponent's attack

For example: You have the ball and you maintain control of it by ingeniously maneuvering your body between the ball and the opponent.

Spills and falls (with or without opponent interference) during routine one-on-one contests

For example: It can happen that you will "fall flat on your face" and then need to get back up on your feet again quickly to continue play. By so doing, you might even be able to prevent another goal.

 Jumping for a high volley, turning in the air and landing without injury

 Reacting quickly to an opponent sprinting away

Quick getaway from an opponent, despite tight marking

A player should be able to control his body exceptionally well so that he will also be able to control the ball and the opponent.

He has to be as swift as a weasel, as cunning as a fox, as alert as a panther, and as strong as a lion.

This is one way you could practice the concerted ensemble of arms, legs and feet!

You will find some better exercises for soccer on the next few pages.

Ideas for practicing excellent coordination

The best way to practice your coordination is, of course, by playing soccer. But there are also other exercises you can do. These are especially good for the wintertime when you are training inside.

Gymnastics

- *tumbling forwards and backwards*
- *handstand and headstand*
- *vaulting (straddling, squatting)*
- *bar exercises (half-circle and circle swings)*
- *back and forth across the monkey bars*

Workout exercises

- *stretching and strengthening your muscles*
- *strengthening stomach and back muscles*
- *relaxation exercises*
- *foot exercises*

Mini-games

- *relay races*
- *team-tag relays*
- *tag games*
- *catching games*

Other games

- *basketball*
- *volleyball*
- *ball over/under a rope*
- *shuttlecock/badminton*
- *tennis*

Other sports

- *swimming*
- *skiing*
- *track and field (triathlon, throwing, sprinting, long jumping)*

Dexterity course
Set up a circuit course with different stations. Who can get through it without making any blunders? Who can get through it the fastest?

Here is just one example of what your course could look like:
balance across a beam – forward roll – crawl under a bench – scale and then jump off wall bars – toss a ball into a basket – run through a maze complex – scramble over an obstacle – rope skipping ten times – throw a medicine ball over a line.

Special soccer exercises for training coordination ability:

Reaction skill

- *Play with only 1-2 ball touches*
  (trap and pass that is all you have time for).

- *Goal kicking exercises against an opponent by sprinting to the ball*
  Who can react the fastest to a sign from the coach and shoot first?

Orientation skill

- *Technique drills like passing, taking the ball on, headers combined with turns, jumps, rolls.*

  e.g.: Throw the ball up. While it is still high in the air above you, make a fast forward roll, leap to your feet, and get control of the ball back – all before it hits the ground.

Balancing skill

- *Guide the ball along while hopping on one leg and passing or shooting it with the other.*

- *Guide the ball while balancing it across a long bench.*

Rhythmic skill

- Dribble the ball with different parts of your foot, zigzagging it to the left and right in front of you. At the same time, softly repeat a rhythm to yourself (1-2-3; 1-2-3).

Differentiation skill

- Practice passing, shooting, dribbling, playing or juggling with balls of different sizes and weights.

- Practice on different types of surfaces like sand, grass, wooden floors or artificial turf.

- From time to time, also play with different kinds of balls like rugby balls, tennis balls or softballs.

Ability to combine motions / Coupling skill

- Practice different techniques in combination with one another (dribble – feint – scoring); switch feet (training the weaker foot).

Special tip:
Excercise faster footwork by jumping and running over poles or through cones or tires. This practices quick reaction skills and coordination of your legs and feet.

You will find some exercises for this on the next page.

Exercise suggestions:

- *Set up small hurdles (even just poles positioned on the ground are good) and run and leap between them – forwards, sideways and backwards.*

- *Build a course out of tires (old bicycle tires make an excellent course and do not cost anything) and run/leap through them on the balls of your feet in a fast manner. Imagine that the tires are hot burners (like on the top of the stove) and you have to get through them super fast.*

- *Practice touching each tire with a different foot (e.g., only one or both feet per tire, or alternate 1, 2 or 1,2,3,2,1,2,3,2,1).*

Special routine for the highly skilled:

Put 6 tires down one behind the other (gym floor or grass).
Master this difficult coordination task:

Tire 1: Jump in with both feet close together, arms to the side
Tire 2: Jump in with feet apart, arms up
Tire 3: Jump in with both feet close together, arms to the side
Tire 4: Jump in with feet apart, arms up
Tire 5: Jump in with both feet close together, arms to the side
Tire 6: Jump in with feet apart, arms up

Those who can master this exercise have excellent coordination and concentration abilities!

Make up your own combination of running, jumping, hopping exercises (with your arms in various different positions), even holding or bouncing a ball at the same time, too. Practice them at home and then show your team and coach during training.

Tips for training technique

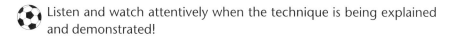
Listen and watch attentively when the technique is being explained and demonstrated!

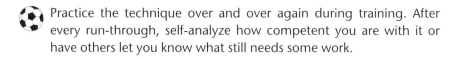
Practice the technique over and over again during training. After every run-through, self-analyze how competent you are with it or have others let you know what still needs some work.

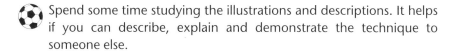
Spend some time studying the illustrations and descriptions. It helps if you can describe, explain and demonstrate the technique to someone else.

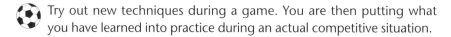
Try out new techniques during a game. You are then putting what you have learned into practice during an actual competitive situation.

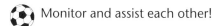
Monitor and assist each other!

How long a soccer player needs to practice in order to learn a new technique is the same as learning new things in school – everyone is different. But we all need to have plenty of practice. In the end, the technique should be executed quickly, cleanly and without any thought to performing its sequence, meaning it has to be completely automatic.

Repetitive training acts to program and store these sequences in your brain. Similar to loading a new computer program that you can always call up again later on.

If you do not make an effort during training, or keep repeating the exercises slowly and/or incorrectly, it will be the slow and faulty sequences which will end up being stored in your brain. Nor will you know any better later on, during some fast-paced match. And all because you allowed something wrong to become automated in the first place.

Monitor – Evaluate – Improve

Do not learn something wrong and let it become automatic! It is vital for you to review the sequence of a new technique and nip mistakes in the bud. How fast this process goes will also depend on your aims and motivation. Remember?

Max learns the header. He has paid attention and intends to heed everything the coach said. Max gives it his all. The coach watches him for a while and then exclaims, "Great, Max! You already seem to have got it!" Max is delighted and continues to practice even more. A few training sessions later, the coach is watching him again (this time he is doing jumping drills) and comments, "You need to work on that some more! You are jumping too late and you are not coiling your body tight enough!" Boy, does that tick Max off! He was doing his headers exactly the same way as that other day when the coach praised him. Yet today, Coach is getting on his back.

You have probably already realized that the coach in this story did not make any mistake. He only adapted his value judgment to the present situation based on the possibilities.

Max's header was in no way perfect during that first training. But for a first attempt, it was very good, very gutsy. Later, after much repetition, improvement should certainly be expected. The next sub-aim should have been reached.

On your way to quick and precise technique, you will achieve many aims and each tiny mistake will be noted and corrected. The assessments your coach will make are the best ones you will ever receive, because he or she is very knowledgeable about soccer and its techniques.

Self-monitoring – self-evaluating

But since the coach cannot be watching everyone at the same time, you will often be training without anyone else looking on checking your progress. Concentrate on turning the coach's instructions and tips into reality for the long run.

Listen closely to what your coach tells you and make mental notes of his or her tips.

First of all, you should get a precise idea of the new technique. Looking at illustrations and watching the coach demonstrate it can help you do this. Whenever you get the chance, watch older and better players in their own training and in actual matches.

Compare the correct execution of the technique with your own and figure out where you might be differing. You will then be aware of the mistakes that you still have to weed out. Keep in mind the mistakes your coach has already criticized.

Set aims for yourself when you train. When you feel you are doing well, go ahead and give yourself a pat on the back for once! But do not hesitate to scold yourself either if you keep on making the same mistake over and over again.

·······························6 TACTICS

What is meant by tactics

Tactics refer to a methodical procedure employed to reach a certain aim. It encompasses not only the procedure itself, but also the means you will call up to perform it.

Recognize yourself?

Max got a bad grade in a test and he has to somehow break this news to his mother.

First, though, he cleans up his room, takes out the trash, and helps his mother set the table. In passing, he mentions the failed test. Just by chance he happens to have it right there in his pocket! A pen for her to sign it as well.

Fortunately she did not go ballistic on him!

Sound familiar? It should, it is only normal. Anyone looking to gain something seeks out the most favorable situation and waits for the right moment. You work up to asking for a bigger allowance or a new CD. In a nutshell – you are proceeding tactically.

Tactics in soccer

Do you remember your first game or even your very first attempts at playing soccer? Remember how all of you ran wildly after the ball? You were all recklessly helter-skelter fixed on that little round object, like a bunch of chickens scrabbling for a grain of corn. Everyone wanted to have the ball all to himself and no game ever came into being!

But you are no longer such a beginner, you are training regularly now in a club, part of a team. You want to play a correct, controlled game and interact well with your teammates. That means spurning the pecking chaos of the chicken coop and welcoming a tactically-played game.

Tactics – Blueprint for victory

Tactics are the procedure or the strategic plan a team has, including the tasks assigned to each player, for potentially defeating a match opponent. We distinguish between team tactics and the tactics for individual players at specific positions.

For a team's tactics, it is vitally important that all players know what they have to do at their positions and what their main job consists of. Not everyone can be scoring goals at the same time. When your side loses the ball, there also has to be players responsible for preventing goals against you. Before each game, and together with the whole team, your coach will work out a "secret pact" for defeating your opponents.

This includes:

- *The objective of the game (normally victory!)*
- *The actions of the team as a whole*
- *The behavior and job of each individual based on the position he is playing*

Paul shoots at goal although he is not in the least in a good position for it. Max dribbles in front of his own goal, loses the ball and the opponent easily pops it into the net. Phillip does not mark his opponent, making it easy for him to dribble at goal.

What was going on here? There was no pre-established order to the team's play. They will go on to lose this match, because everybody is just doing what they feel like and there is no actual game being played.

Who plays what position is something that is decided before a match ever starts. Many different game formations have been established in this regard. The two illustrations shows the 4-3-3; and the 3-4-3 formation for playing 11 vs. 11 on a regulation pitch.

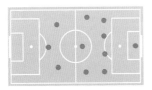 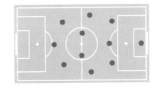

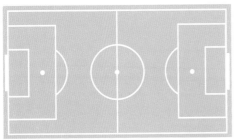

What does your starting formation look like? Draw the line-up here.

Tactic training

Tactical training from your coach will teach and drill into you that ...

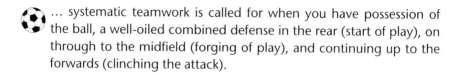 ... systematic teamwork is called for when you have possession of the ball, a well-oiled combined defense in the rear (start of play), on through to the midfield (forging of play), and continuing up to the forwards (clinching the attack).

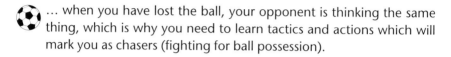 ... when you have lost the ball, your opponent is thinking the same thing, which is why you need to learn tactics and actions which will mark you as chasers (fighting for ball possession).

... soccer is played by position or positional groups, and not keeping to these means forfeiting fine-tuned teamwork.

... soccer is a one-on-one contest. The one-on-one play gives the concept of team versus team for victory or defeat at its most basic fundamental level. One-on-one showdowns are the smallest unit of a soccer game and victory normally goes to whichever side wins the most of them. This is why it is so important that players approach such one-on-one challenges boldly and with full commitment.

... when you have lost the ball, you have to employ fair means to get it back and use skillful tactics when pitting yourself against the opponent in possession of it (fakes/feints).

So you will not get overloaded trying to practice everything all at once. Your coach will help you focus on certain main highlights during your training. You can also practice and drill your own technical-tactical actions as well.

Serious orderly soccer matches call not only for your technical skills, but also for a basic underlying tactical approach, which you will learn as you go along and which, as a whole, is what ultimately distinguishes a soccer team from a bunch of pecking chickens.

What tactical tips could the coach give his players here? Fill in the balloons yourself!

61

What a soccer player needs to learn about tactical behavior

Play without the ball / Marking

- Triangle formation ensures two play possibilities for the player with the ball.
- Run toward the player with the ball.
- Run into an open space away from being marked.
- Do not run on ahead, tearing away for the ball, without visual contact with the ball and your teammates.
- Do not run around aimlessly behind the player in possession of the ball.
- Teammates who are not being marked determine the moment and direction of a pass.
- As an unmarked player don't run about without taking all the actions of your teammates into account.

Teamwork

- Passing to a better positioned (unmarked) teammate takes precedence over dribbling.
- Run to the left, play to the right and vice-versa.
- Play the ball to your teammate while he is running or directly onto his foot.
- The play near or behind the opponent dictates a teammate's route.
- Never play across the penalty area but always away from your own goal.
- Combine dribbling with evading maneuvers and feinting.

Scoring goals

- Complete every attack whenever possible with a shot at goal.
- Shoot from all positions, but not too hastily and provided there is enough room.
- Combine goal attempts with evading maneuvers and feinting.

One-on-one conduct

- Try to hustle the oppunent as soon as he receives the ball.
- Mark the inner line.
- After gaining possession of the ball, play it immediately to unmarked teammates or dribble into an open space.
- Switch to defense immediately upon losing the ball (attempt to win the ball back).
- The closer you are to the goal, the tighter the opponents' marking and cover.
- Do not overdo the dribbling. Try to keep your dribbling down to those times when there is no teammate next to or in front of you, when they are all marked, or you only have one opponent in front of you and enough room.

Learn these important points for your tactical play right at the beginning of your soccer career. Of course, just like when you are learning technique, you will not be able to digest all of them at once. This, too, is a step-by-step process. Only those who persevere in their training will be the ones who keep getting better and better.

- Whenever possible, win the first one-on-one.
- Whenever possible, play the first pass on to a teammate.
- Always go with your first instinct.
- Hustle the opponent as soon as he touches the ball.
- Do not attack an opponent too hastily, do not make the first move.
- Never play crosswise to or through the penalty area, crossing passes always away from opponent.
- Cover the inner line.
- Passing takes precedence over dribbling.
- If the situation demands, then use this to dribble with feints and a successful one-on-one.
- When attacking, dribble swiftly, never come to a standstill.
- Get your body between the ball and an opponent.
- Defense = high security and low risk.
- Attack = high risk and less security.

So what's your trick when you are standing there in front of the net with the ball?

That's easy!
Tom holds on to the goalie, Alfie grapples with the defenders, and Mark throws himself at all the rest.
So I have all the time in the world to sink it!

What are your thoughts on that?

Tactics for each position

Defense

The team's defensive department. The specific job defense performs includes marking, preventing opponent goals, and cutting off forwards. In today's soccer, if defenders gain possession of the ball, they are also involved in furthering the game offensively. They will even score goals from time to time.

Defensive variations when marking opposing attackers:

Man marking

Each defensive player marks a particular player who is opposite him on the other team.

Area Cover

Each defensive player is assigned a certain zone he is responsible for covering. He goes after any opponents who enter into his area of co-verage.

Teams which combine both of these variations play the best. Total in-your-face man marking makes no sense, nor does loose area cover. Imprecise allocation of duties and areas leaves a team open to major threat goals being scored against you.

The midfield

The midfield makes or breaks the game. Here is where we find the "brain" or the "engine" of the team. The midfield is responsible for forging or advancing its own game, setting up the attacks on the opposing goal, and also for supporting the defense upon attack by the opponent.

This is where the most technically adept, most tactically shrewd and strongest, most fit players are deployed. They need to be constantly ready to jump into the fray at a split second's notice, be able to skillfully dummy round and mislead an opponent. Their long shots make them formidable scoring threats themselves, and they will think nothing of racking up great distances rushing forward and backward. Michael Ballack exemplifies such an excellent midfielder. Any team would be thrilled to have him in their ranks.

Nowadays, on a regulation pitch, the midfield is positioned as a chain of four or five. In past years, it was also a row with 3 players (one at the right, one in the center and one at the left). On smaller fields (small-sided play of 7 on 7 or 8 on 8), a team should make use of, for example, three midfield players. One plays right, one center as a key anchor (both offensive and defensive), and one left. The two outside players have the task of supporting their team's attacks as well as its defense and to bring the game forward along the outer flanks.

The attack

Attackers represent the offensive department of a team and they are particularly responsible for scoring goals. Goals guarantee victory – they are the icing on every game. Not only would soccer be a really boring game if there were no goals, it would definitely be far less popular. This is also why a team's fans seem to especially idolize their scorers and forwards. Forwards do not have it easy today, because they are usually playing under very relentless and closley marked. They need to counter-act that by being strong dribblers, highly confident with the ball, feinting

experts, plus very, very fast in eluding their opponents. A good forward needs to have the so-called *goal instinct*. That means crisp, cool intuitive shots at the net, swiftly making use of every chance that comes up, and always being at the right place at the right time whenever the opportunity to score comes up. But forwards also have defensive duties. As soon as a player loses a ball, everyone switches back immediately to defense. The whole team abruptly switches from offense to defense. In this sense, by fighting to get the ball back, while still in the opponent's half, the forwards are the first main line of defense. In today's modern soccer, this is referred to as *pressing* or *forechecking*.

Youth soccer should always make use of three forwards; i.e., one outside-right, one in the middle as center-forward, and one outside-left. It is the job of the two outside forwards (wingers) to make attacks up their flank and to pass across inwards, threatening the goal. The center-forward or other midfielder or defender moving up the pitch remains alert to any scoring opportunity.

Center-forwards have the job of shooting goals or making headers out of every slightest chance. They keep the defense busy and on their toes. When a center-forward is marked too tightly, he will also slip away rearward or out on the wings in order to make room for others in the middle.

Set play situations are also a part of your tactics

These are the actions which follow when ...
.... the ball goes out *(throw-in, corner kick, goal kick)*
.... the referee stops play for a foul *(free kick, penalty kick)*
.... the game is started or restarted after half-time or after a goal has
     been scored *(kickoff)*

Set play situations come up over and over again in every game and are therefore the norm for a soccer match. They are also somewhat special because the ball was always at rest or out of the game beforehand!

....7 FITNESS

Max goes to the doctor because he thinks there might be something physically wrong with him. "I do not know what is wrong with me, Doctor! After our last training game, I was totally exhausted. I was really dizzy and almost fainted, I had a bad cramp in my calf, and my arms and my legs were aching something awful."

"Sounds like you did not train enough!"

"But I do! I go to training three times a week. And I always practice my kicking technique, trapping and dribbling there."

Can you guess what the doctor will probably tell Max next? Of course! That he forgot his fitness. That is why he has no stamina or strength and why his joints are so stiff and unforgiving. His body has never got used to the constant running that can last for as long as two halves.

What we mean by fitness

The term *condition* refers primarily to your physical abilities. Your condition determines just how fit you are, what kind of endurance or stamina you have, or exactly how much exertion you can handle. You will be able to tell how good your condition is (or is not) by how out of breath you get after a short run, how long you can keep up with athletic exertion without your legs starting to ache, or how quickly you tire. Apart from your soccer training, you can also improve your condition by playing other kinds of sports, including school sports.

S	P	E	E	D	S	K	A	T	I	N	G	C	V	W	E
A	R	D	T	G	W	L	L	A	B	D	N	A	H	O	B
Y	T	G	A	R	I	Y	G	N	I	Z	L	O	P	R	I
R	B	N	O	R	M	I	K	M	R	S	A	Z	J	V	F
T	A	I	B	Y	M	P	H	C	Q	U	M	L	O	F	U
N	P	E	N	S	I	N	N	E	T	M	A	P	G	H	N
U	P	O	A	Z	N	T	I	B	G	Y	R	N	G	A	Y
O	L	N	F	I	G	O	R	E	S	K	A	T	I	N	G
C	K	A	I	H	U	V	D	J	B	T	T	O	N	D	H
S	O	C	J	P	P	Y	S	F	V	Y	H	O	G	B	O
S	V	D	M	O	Y	W	M	L	O	E	O	U	B	A	T
O	S	P	E	E	D	W	A	L	K	I	N	G	I	L	K
R	O	C	K	C	L	I	M	B	I	N	G	R	W	L	A
C	R	W	D	L	E	I	F	D	N	A	K	C	A	R	T

Find eleven sports which require stamina and which you can practice in addition to soccer to train your own stamina. We have hidden them horizontally and vertically, and both forward and backward.

Fitness ability

We can easily identify the individual elements that together make up the fit condition a soccer player needs to have in order to be in all-round good shape: stamina, speed and strength. Let us look at each of these a little more closely now.

Stamina

Stamina is the prerequisite an athlete needs for handling continued exertion over long periods of time without tiring too quickly. Those who have good stamina can keep up their pace for long periods of time in the face of physical exertion, they are physically fit, they will recover faster after training and matches, and they can concentrate longer. During a soccer match, you are running virtually non-stop, with constant sprints thrown in for good measure.

Off the soccer field, you can train your stamina by doing endurance runs. You should run for at least fifteen minutes, two to three times per week, either at an even tempo or a varied one. Other excellent stamina sports include cycling, skipping with a rope, inline skating, ball games, hockey, winter sports and all variations of soccer and football.

Speed

Speed is the ability you need to execute a movement or motion with the ideal acceleration and swiftness. You want to be like a flash of lightning when on the heels of an opponent or running away with the ball. It is the fastest sprinter who usually wins the one-on-one contests or is the first to the ball, cutting off the opposing forward.

When you are training, your actions and movements have to be fast. If you only train halfheartedly, you will not be any faster during an actual match either.

Strength

Strength is required for moving something heavy, – for instance, when you are lifting, thrusting, pulling or pushing a heavy weight – including your own body! You need strength in your legs for kicking goals, for fast sprints and for jumping high into a header. Playing soccer itself is an ideal way to train your strength. But you have also got many more opportunities off the soccer field using devices like elastic bands or even just your own body weight.

You actually do not need any special gear for simple strengthening exercises. The weight of your own body will suffice for exercises such as push-ups, sit-ups, knee bends or skipping with a rope.

This book also includes a number of other exercises you can do with or without extra accessories.

Exercising with an elastic band

Many soccer players swear by this quite simple but wonderfully all-purpose sports equipment for increasing their strength. This roughly 50" x 6" elastic band is not expensive and it takes up very little room – it will fit in any gym bag. You can find such an elastic band under a number of different product names from various manufacturers.

Here are some sample exercises. Do not forget to warm up first!

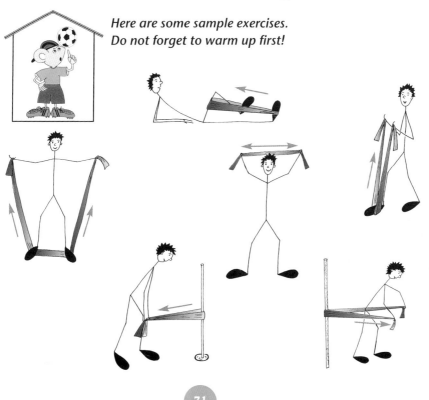

How would you rate your own stamina, sprint speed, jumping strength and agility? Playing soccer actually provides you with the best, most varied training you can get.

But you can also do some additional exercises off the field.

 ### Distance running

Pick a set distance of about a mile. If you want to know the exact distance, you can measure it with a bicycle or automobile odometer. But it is fine if you just want to make a rough estimate. The distance can, of course, also be longer. What is most important for monitoring your performance is that you run exactly the same distance every time. Jot down your time once a week.

 ### Sprinting exercises

When you are out jogging, add some short sprints to your normal steady pace. Look for trees, road signs or intersections as your start and finish lines. Run the distance between them as fast as you can.

Mark off a distance of about 10-30 yards on the sidewalk or on a quiet street (be sure you will be able to find your marks again later on!). Find a helper who'll time your sprints and give you a starting signal.

Jumps

This exercise improves the explosive strength to your leg and hip muscles. Start with slightly bent knees and then, with a powerful swing of your arms, jump as high and as far as you can.

Reach leap (high-speed strength)
Stand on the balls of your feet against a wall or post. Raise your arms as high as you can and mark the spot you can reach with a piece of tape or chalk. Now jump with both legs as forcefully as you can – and straight up vertically (maximum height).

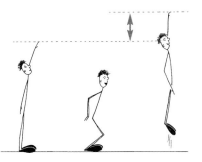

Mark your jump height at the highest point you can reach with your hand. (If you are practicing alone, hold something like a piece of chalk in your hand and mark the spot as you jump. Just stay away from the expensive wallpaper in the living room or your neighbor's prized white-washed wall!) The difference between the height you can reach by stretching and your jump height is your jump rating.

 Push-ups (strength/arms)
Your arms extend out from your shoulders and your body. Place a thin pillow or a mat under your face. Do the push-ups one right after the other (non-stop), remembering that your chin should always touch the pillow each time.

 Sit-ups (strength/abdomen)
Lie on your back with your hands cradled behind your neck and your legs bent 90º. Raise your body upright and then lower it again in a continuous non-stop rhythm.

Additional training

Make sure your training does not get bogged down in a rut – you need a balanced training plan. Discuss it with your coach. A soccer player develops an impressive muscular body, but he is not a bodybuilder. Most successful players work on their fitness at home in addition to their set training sessions.

Write down the additional exercises you do here. Check off how frequently you do them! You will surely also get "homework" from your coach.

	rarely	once a week	daily
Strength			
Stamina			
Speed			

Tracking your personal performance

You can also review your performance yourself from time to time, too. This is a lot of fun to do, because if you are putting everything you have got into your training, you will see how your results (usually!) improve each time. The results from your exercises can be easily depicted in a chart, just like all your other training drills and match results. You have probably already learned how to do diagram charts in a maths or physics class. If you are having a hard time setting it all up at first, there is bound to be someone you know, to whom you can go for help.

Use a square-ruled notebook (graph paper would be even better) to draw your diagrams. You can make the time units along the x-axis weeks or months. The units along the y-axis (seconds, repetitions or inches, etc.) depend upon the discipline you will be tracking.

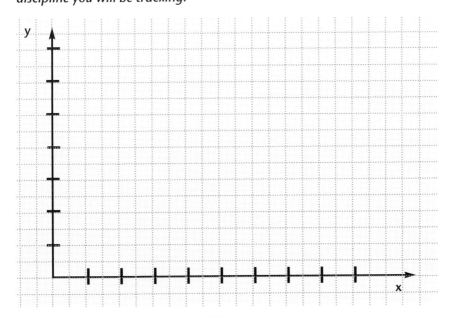

Warm up – Stretching – Loosening up

Regardless of whether you begin to train by doing exercises at home, or whether there is a match – this rule always applies! It is important that you get your body ready for the exertion. After a long day at school or a restful sleep, your muscles are still relatively cold and stiff, your breathing and pulse rate set at "normal mode." When you are facing a training session or a game, you have to get your whole body ready gradually. Then, by the time that the first whistle blows, your "motor is already revved up" and you can take off at full power.

Warming up

Just like it sounds – you warm your body up! A varied routine of fast-paced exercises increases the blood flowing to your muscles, allowing them to perform better. Signs of this warmed-up state include feeling looser and more limber, a slight reddening to your skin and light sweating. Warming up properly helps prevent injuries like pulled muscles and sprains.

All activity, which really gets you going, makes for good warm-up exercises: *running, light jumps, aerobics, ball games, relay races or informal play.*

Muscle stretching

Flexibility and mobility are primarily improved by stretching your muscles. Stretching greatly expands the muscle group you are working.

Here are some exercises for stretching the muscles used in soccer. Can you feel them working? Have fun!

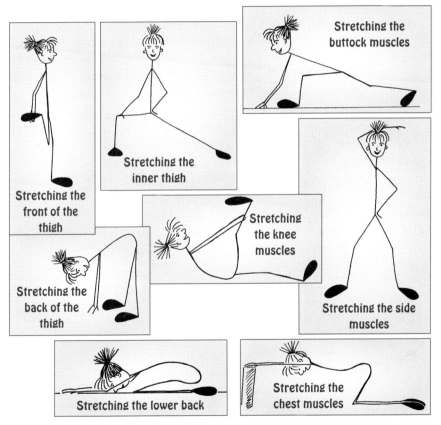

Stretching the buttock muscles

Stretching the inner thigh

Stretching the front of the thigh

Stretching the knee muscles

Stretching the back of the thigh

Stretching the side muscles

Stretching the lower back

Stretching the chest muscles

Count to 20 during each stretch, relax your muscles, and then repeat. No bouncing! These exercises are designed to stretch your muscles – they should never hurt!

Loosening up

Even after sufficient warming up and stretching, muscles are often stiff and tight after an exhausting training session. That is why after the final stretching, it is necessary to loosen yourself up. Usually we do these kinds of exercises automatically. We shake out our arms, legs, hands and gently move our joints in all directions. Slow-paced running or jumping can also serve to loosen one up.

But this time you spend preparing for an athletic contest involves more than just warming up your muscles and getting your whole body going. It also entails psyching yourself up mentally for the coming challenge.

Shake off all your worries and problems, clear your head, and make yourself open and receptive to whatever comes your way.

The Soccer Player's Warm-up program

You already know how important a thorough warm-up is before training and especially before a match. It is ideal if all players on a team can run through the same warm-up program together right before the game starts. It is not only more fun that way, it also serves to unite all of you as one team. Prepare as a team because you want to win as a team!

What a warm-up program might look like:

Exercises for warming up the whole body
- *running, gymnastics, stretching exercises*
- *short sprints, varied-pace runs*

5 min

Group exercises with the ball
- *passing with the inside of the foot in a circle while changing positions*
- *double passes, short pass sequences and longer passes in pairs*

7 min

Exercises in match-like situations
- *5 against 5 or as open play on a downsized playing field*

5 min

Relaxing as a group
- *stretching exercises*
- *ritual*

2 min

A lot of teams have a common ritual at the end of their warm-ups, right before the starting whistle. They huddle into a circle with their arms around each other's shoulders and roar out a chant. Do you have something like that, too? How does it go?

...............8 MENTAL CAPABILITY

What makes us as human beings feel joy and grief, fall in love or develop bitter hate for someone else?

How is it that we can think and remember, dream and imagine?

People have always wanted to know just what exactly was going on inside our heads. Because we could not explain it, we simply called the whole thing our *soul*. The famous physician Rudolf Virchow (1821-1902) once asked his students to find the soul within the human body. What they found within the cadavers they dissected was the brain, the heart, the lungs, the liver and all the other organs. But no soul. It would have been impossible to find it anyway, because our perceptions and observations, our thoughts and our decisions as well as our feelings and desires, all result from the unseen activity going on in our brain. The branch of science which studies such phenomena is called *psychology* and the old term of the '*soul*' has since been replaced by the word *psyche*.

Mental capability thus refers to how a soccer player handles joy, aggravation, anger, excitement, the will to win and all the many other feelings he will experience, and how he puts them to use successfully and to his own advantage during training and matches. Psychology also studies how our thinking process works and how our muscles receive orders. Just imagine your brain is a powerful computer controlling everything. During a soccer match, your "computer" runs at top speed, but it also needs to be well-trained in order to do so.

What does the inside of our "computer" look like?

It is not our intent to write a medical textbook here. Besides, the brain is far too complicated and extensive an object to describe in just one short chapter. But there are some people who truly believe that a sport only has to do with our muscles. They do not realize that the impulses for the muscles come from the brain or that each and every complicated movement an athlete performs is actually controlled by the nerve connections within our brain. So that you will recognize the important role your brain plays while you are out there on the field, we felt it was imperative to include a chapter like this in our training book.

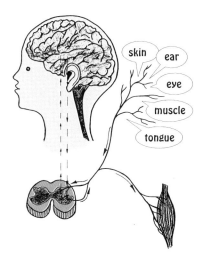

skin ear

eye

muscle

tongue

Conscious reactions

Information comes in through our sense organs. You see something, or hear it, taste it or touch it. This information is then forwarded to the brain over neural pathways. After a control check is made on the incoming impulse, it is compared with past experiences and processed intellectually. Commands sent back to the muscles over the neural pathways go through the spinal cord (acting like a coordinating switching station).

Game Tips

Win the first one-on-one whenever possible
- This gives you self-confidence.
- It weakens your opponent's self-confidence.
- Gets you respect right from the very start.

Reaction to a goal
- Joy, jubilation, embracing – enjoy the triumph!
- Your teamwork and the outcome it brought about was a spectacular success. You played right though the defense and the goalie. Keep up the good work!
- Do not get too cocky! Quickly shift back to defense and concentrate on a new attack.

Reactions to an opponent's goal
- Something went wrong with the defense.
- Say to yourself: "Doesn't matter!" or "Don't worry!" or even: "Now we'll really get down to business."
- Their goal is definitely an aggravation, but the game is not over until the final whistle blows. Anything and everything can and will still happen.

When your stamina starts to taper off
- During a long game, you will experience low points where your legs start to feel very heavy and your strength seems to be fading away. Don't give up!
- Overcome your weakness and muster all your energy up to the final whistle.
- Remember that your opponents are getting tired, too.

Watch how top-rated players chill out and concentrate before a match, or when substituted, or when their side scores, or when the opponent scores. Try to imitate them and find out what works best for you. Practice these rituals and perform them over and over again.

Emotional strength

Some say, "Self-confidence is half the battle!" Naturally it is not quite that simple but there is a good deal of truth in that saying. He or she who is self-confident, full of enthusiasm and approaches each situation absolutely raring to go, will of course have better chances of success than another person who may be timid or full of doubt.

But do not take your self-confidence to the level where you get so cocky that you start to make mistakes!

Give me a break! This game is a piece of cake for me! After all, I am the best around! Why did you clowns even show up today in the first place?

Ohh, I am going to blow it again, I just know it. I am just too weak. I only have to see the other guys and I am ready to run back home again!

Which of the following qualities and attitudes are helpful to a soccer player and which ones are more self-defeating? Cross out the ones you'd rather not have too much of.

Self-esteem – Having fun when playing – Self-doubt – Blind rage – Willingness to take risks – Laid-back approach – Fear of making a mistake – Ambition – Will to win – Confidence in your own performance – Pessimism – Bad mood – Feeling in good shape – Ability to concentrate

Prerequisites for a successful game

Peak physical state
You have trained well, you feel strong, laid-back, relaxed and pumped up with energy. You have a good feeling, you are a little excited, but not apprehensive or nervous.

Peak mental state
You are looking forward to the game and to winning it together with your team. You are confident you will reach the aims you have set for yourself, yet you are not afraid of defeat either.

Winner attitude
You have got a positive and optimistic mindset. When you lose a ball or a one-on-one confrontation, no moaning, "Now the whole day is ruined!" Instead, say to yourself: "I want to score and I want my team to win. Nothing's ever over until that final whistle blows."

Winner posture
Take another look at those two figures on Page 84. Who do you think is more likely to see victory? The one with the erect, self-confident posture, of course. Show the others that you have unwavering confidence in yourself, even when things go wrong!

Even the best soccer player loses every now and then

When you lose a one-on-one, or an opponent takes you down a peg or two, or you can never seem to get anything past that goalie, you have to take a moment to ask yourself why. Maybe the opponents were older than you. If so, they have been training longer than you have and are therefore stronger. Should this be the case, do not get all het up about it, just keep on training. If you are good, you will catch up with them at some point. Be pleased with your own personal best.

If you feel you should have had a little more in you, then think about the reasons and causes.

Writing down a synopsis of the reasons behind lackluster performances can help.

Times I was unsatisfied with my game	What were the reasons?	What I want to do about it in the near future
August 3 – match against Modesto	*I lost the ball a lot.*	*Practice my dribbling.*
September 22 – match against Albany	*I was completely exhausted during the second half.*	*Be more active in training games, do more endurance runs.*

Self-imposed pressure builds emotional strength

What do you think after reading Max's story? Sound a little familiar?

> *Max had really looked forward to the game. He told everyone how good his training was going and that the coach was putting him into the next game. He had his bag all packed the night before, and everything marked off on his checklist. All that was left was early to bed to sleep to be fit for the big day! But then he lost every single one-on-one, his passes always came up too short, and he even came within a hair of causing a penalty kick. Everyone was bewildered that day, wondering whatever could be wrong with Max. Unfortunately, the coach was ultimately forced to take him off.*

What happened to Max can even happen to famous professional players facing important games. The pressure was simply too much, he was too excited, he could not muster up his true abilities.

While it does not signal the end of an entire career, it is frustrating. You should know why such situations arise and what you can do about them.

Pressure is related to expectations

There are some expectations which come from others.

Bravo, you are the best!
We are so proud of you!
You are going to score the winning goal today!
Show them what you got!
I'm relying on you!

They come from your parents, your coach and your friends.

They are all expecting you to perform well.

We are going to win today!
I am going to show all of you!
I am going to score a goal!
Everyone will be proud and cheer!
All that training has finally paid off!

And then there are those expectations you place on yourself. You set your own aims that you want to reach.

Sometimes the pressure these expectations exert gets to be too much. You get scared that you will not be able to meet the high expectations others have of you, or those you have placed on yourself. And that is stressful!

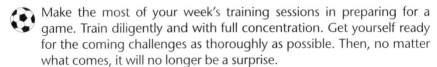

Coming to terms with pressure

Make the most of your week's training sessions in preparing for a game. Train diligently and with full concentration. Get yourself ready for the coming challenges as thoroughly as possible. Then, no matter what comes, it will no longer be a surprise.

Go to sleep early, set everything out the night before, have a good breakfast, and leave home in plenty of time.

Push all your problems, unrelated to the game, out of your mind. Put up a mental force field so that no external problems can weasel in while you are out on the field. Concentrate only on your opponents, your teammates, the ball and the game.

Subjecting yourself to this pressure is actually something you yourself have chosen to do! You have set your own aims and you decide for yourself what you plan on accomplishing. Of course, you can always take the pressure off yourself by settling for goals much easier to attain. Maybe you refuse to enter into any one-on-one contests, or you let all your other teammates attempt goals, or maybe you even stay on the sideline the whole time keeping the bench warm. But how logical does that sound? It is better to set high but still realistic aims. A little bit of pressure is not only inevitable, it is crucial. That is what makes the whole thing fun. It is what spurs us on and keeps us going.

Pressure builds character! You only become strong by coping with pressure situations. And each time you do, you become that much more resilient and more adept at handling them. He or she who is already avoiding pressure as early as the preparatory stages becomes a "weakling", forever to remain an underachiever, while those who can overcome themselves build character.

The character traits you cultivate in training and in playing will also benefit you in other areas of your life. You will be able to cope better with homework and tests – not to mention all the other difficult situations life will throw your way.

Test your mental capabilities

How would you react in the following situations?

Situation 1: **You are just not in the mood to go to training.**

A. Of course you stay at home; one should never be forced to do anything against their own will.   1

B. You head off for the soccer field rather unenthusiastically. After all you really do not want to disappoint your parents.   2

C. You head for training like always, because whenever you miss a session your performance suffers the next time around. And who knows, you just might perk up by the time you hit the field.   3

Situation 2: **The coach keeps criticizing your first touch.**

A. It sure is frustrating that it has not fallen into place yet, but first you want to practice your goal shots before anything else.   2

B. Why is he always being so petty? It is like he thinks this is a beauty pageant or something! One more word out of him and you'll clear off.   1

C. It is good that the coach is always watching so closely. That way you will never train using the wrong technique in the first place.   3

Situation 3: **Your team was awarded a penalty kick. You are supposed to make it. You are now at the penalty spot and getting the ball placed right.**

A. You are fully concentrated, breathing normally, and reflecting on how and where you should kick the ball.   3

B. You are thinking what a scoring superstar you are today. Of course you glance around to see if all your relatives are there – you even give them all a big wave.   2

C. You are scared you are going to blow the whole thing. After all, it is pre-programed that the goalkeeper will pounce on it. It is clear you do not stand a chance against him.   1

Situation 4: **You are not picked for the line-up this time and instead have to cool your heels on the bench.**

A. You think what bad luck, maybe I am not good enough. 2

B. You are fuming because you know you are at least as good as the others. You are now rooting for the other team to win so yours will realize that they need you. 1

C. You cheer your team on, besides, there is still time possibly to be called in later. You make a vow you will really give it your all during the next training session. 3

....

Situation 5: **Your team goes down a goal against the opponents.**

A. As expected, the other team is simply much stronger than yours. 1

B. Now you really turn on the gas so that your team can tie it up quickly. We can still make anything happen out there; we are all very well-trained. 3

C. Time to heighten our defense and try to keep them from scoring too many more. 2

....

Situation 6: **A teammate fakes a dramatic headlong dive into the box and despite a fair one-on-one, your team is awarded a penalty kick.**

A. You lecture him about unsportsmanlike conduct. Your team certainly does not need to resort to tricks in order to win. 3

B. It definitely was not fair, but if the ref did not catch it, all the more reason to cheer. 2

C. Great idea! Obviously the referee is not keeping such close tabs. You are going to try to get away with the same thing the very next chance you get. 1

Add up your score!
You will find an evaluation in the answers section at the back of the book.

Relaxation exercises

To relax, you need to find a quiet place where no one will disturb you. Lie down on a mat or a warm floor. Close your eyes. The most important part is proper breathing:

Breathe deeply into your abdomen, your stomach should rise up like a rounded balloon.

Let your breath out silently and very slowly, your abdominal wall slowly sinking.

The following exercises are for stretching your muscles and tendons. You should feel a slight pull. That is good, as long as it does not hurt. Hold the position for as long as it is comfortable. Do not bounce! Do not forget your good, deep breathing from the abdomen when you are doing these exercises! Yoga books are another great source for these types of exercises.

Make yourself into a little small bundle.

Lying on your back, bring your legs up over and behind your head.

From a kneeling position, arch your back like a cat.

..........................9 SOCCER TRAINING TECHNIQUES AND TACTICS

We want to use this chapter to outline tips and suggestions on how you can train your technique and tactics. It is virtually impossible to consider one separately from the other. When you are out there playing, you always draw upon them as one complete unit, since every time you use a technique, you also have a motive behind it. When we describe important moves for practicing a technique, it is always coupled closely together with tips for tactical behavior during a game. Always practice on technical elements together with an eye on the tactics – with a purpose.

Learning technique is a step-by-step process. We have listed some of them here for you. Learning tactical specifics only really happens by actually using them in a game. So, in addition to training, in order to get the most tactical experience under your belt as possible, you should simply be out there playing a lot.

Those who want to play great soccer, have to learn and practice the most important techniques. These are part and parcel of the "basic tools" of any soccer player. In fact playing the game would not even be possible without them.

Do you recognize the basic techniques portrayed in these drawings? The following pages will explain them in greater detail.

Types of shots

You need different types of shots to get the ball into the goal with your foot or with your head, to pass it to a teammate, or steal it away from an opponent and keep it in play. The player determines the direction, angle, height and distance. So that all this will come together masterfully, you have to know the different types of shots and practice them as often as you can.

You can play the ball with:

• the foot

the heel

the inside
of the foot

the inner instep

the instep

the tip
of the foot

the outside
of the foot

• the head
• the chest, the knee, the thigh

The ball is played:
• into the opposing goal
• to teammates
• into open areas

The ball should not be played:
• into your own goal
• to opponents
• out of play

Different types of shots are presented briefly on the next few pages. If a shot fails, then you did something wrong in performing it. We have listed some common mistakes. Can you relate to any of them? If so, check them off. But do it in pencil – hopefully you will be able to erase them again very soon!

The inside of the foot shot

- for shallow passes over short and medium distances.
- for direct passes (double passes).
- for an accurate and sure shot at goal.

Mistakes you should avoid:

The kicking leg is not swung through straight and the shot "botched", the ball will miss its target.

The toe is not pointing in the direction of play and the support foot is too far away from the ball, the movement is too "angled" and "awkward".

The ankle is not held stiff; you will not hit the ball right at its center.

Practice tips:

- Do some dry runs first to check and note the way you move. However, do not spend too much time on them!
- First practice the inside of the foot shot from a stationary position without run-up.
- Pick out a line, for example a mark on the field, and kick the ball with the inside of your foot so that it rolls straight down your chosen line.
- Set up mini target goals and aim for them from a short distance.
- Kick the ball against a wall with the inside of your foot. As it bounces back off, play it back immediately with the inside of your foot again.

The inner instep kick

- for long, high passes (prolonging a game).
- for cross passes, corner kicks, free kicks.
- for a goal kick after a ball crosses the end line.

The outside of the foot kick

- for chip passes (evading round the opponent).
- for making a goal, corner or free kick.

The instep kick

- for a sharp drive at the goal.
- for a goal kick after a ball crosses the end line.
- for free kicks.

Mistakes you should avoid with instep kicks:

If you are afraid of "scraping" your toes on the ground, you will not hit the ball with your lacings but with just the tips of your toes instead and it will go flying off somewhere at random.

When you do not keep your ankle stiff, you can not hit the ball at its center and you will miss your target.

Your run-up is not straight and not in the direction of the kick.

Your support foot is too far behind the ball.

Your upper body is lagging too far behind.

Special shots

Spin

The ball is given spin when it is hit just off center from the side with the inner or outer instep. It takes on a banana-shaped or curved trajectory around the opponent.

Volley

The ball comes in high and a scorer strikes it before it can touch the ground. Kicks like these, including full instep, pirouettes, sideways lunges or bicycle kicks are very spectacular as they whiz toward the net. Because they come in very fast and crisply, they are unpredictable for the goalie. These are how most of soccer's "amazing goals" are made. Volleys are also excellent techniques in defense, for making long clearance shots away from one's own penalty area, against opponent cross passes and in the face of opponent power play situations.

Drop kick

Here the ball comes in high and briefly touches the ground. The scorer is right on it after it strikes the ground and bangs it back up high into the air with his instep. These shots are also rather sharp and definitely spectacular. If the instep meets the ball perfectly at its center, the goalie usually does not stand a chance.

Suggestions for practicing your kicks

Lining up with the rest of your teammates in training, and simply playing a ball served up to you, one by one, gets boring fairly quickly. Vary the routine by alternating between different kinds of competitive situations which call for precision, power and range. Practice with different balls in order to train your feel for the ball.

We have written down some examples for you here, but your coach will also have a lot of good ideas and you can even think up some different exercises yourself. Have fun!

Kicking at goals
- *of different sizes*
- *from different distances*
- *with different balls*

This will give you an idea of what type of kicks you will need to master as well as the force each one requires.

Competition
- *Who will make the most goals within a predefined number of kicks?*
- *Who will score a goal from the farthest distance?*
- *Who will score the most goals for the other side?*

Threesome

Three players set up a goal (approx. 9 feet wide) and mark a goal-kicking point at the same distance (approx. 30 feet) on both sides.

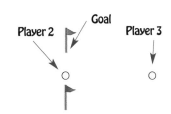

One acts as goalie and the other two are scorers on the two opposite facing sides. Once one of you shoots a goal, it becomes the other player's turn (the ball is heading in his direction anyway!) If the goalie can stop it, he or she changes places with the scorer. Who scores the most goals and who intercepts the most shots?

Target shooting

You will need a goal about 3 feet wide made of cones, poles, or lines on a wall. Mark the goal-kicking point approx. 15 feet back and try to score a goal. Once someone scores, the goal-kicking point is moved three steps backwards and the scorer tries again. If he or she scores again, the point goes back another three steps. Continue until someone misses. They have to stay at that distance until they score a goal.

Who can score from farthest away?

Favorite exercise:

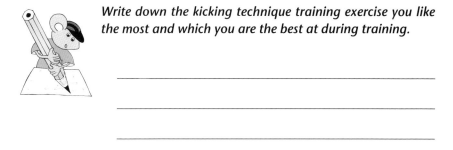

Write down the kicking technique training exercise you like the most and which you are the best at during training.

_____

_____

_____

_____

Always alternate between your left leg and your right leg when practicing your goal-kicking so that you will not become lopsided or "one-sided." You do not want your "weak" leg to turn into a wooden peg that you can only use to support yourself – that is not of any help whatsoever to a soccer player. You can also alternate legs by declaring one week a "right week" and the next one a "left week."

Do not worry that you are neglecting your "strong" leg. On the contrary, it will always be training right along with you... each and every step of the way!

Dribbling and ball control

- *Ball control* refers to the technique where you move the ball along using different parts of your feet without being threatened by an opponent.
- *Dribbling* is guiding the ball under threat of an opponent; i.e. tactical implications.

Soccer is a running game and it thrives on the coordinated teamwork of all teammates. This means it is sometimes necessary to drive the ball some distance ahead of you ("dribble") before passing it on to a teammate or shooting at a goal.

Why is dribbling so helpful in soccer?

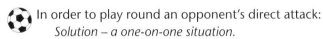 In order to play round an opponent's direct attack:
    Solution – a one-on-one situation.

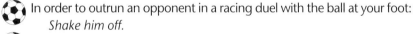 In order to outrun an opponent in a racing duel with the ball at your foot:
    Shake him off.

In order to lure an opponent (dribble toward him) and then time it just right to play the ball off to a teammate:
    Dupe your opponent.

What does dribbling with the ball at your foot really achieve?

It keeps the opponent from gaining possession of the ball, you sell him a dummy. You can play on without a threat. This makes scoring goals much easier because there are fewer opponents defending the goal. They have already either been sold a dummy or outrun.

The greatest names in soccer are usually all very good dribblers. They are extremely skilled at shielding the ball and fending off opponent attacks. Who can you think of? Make a list here!

What can you use to dribble with?

- the inside of the foot
  (cutting off with the inside of the foot)
- the outside of the foot
  (cutting off with the outside of the foot)
- the instep
- the sole
  (using the sole to roll it)

Learn to dribble well! These tips are particularly important for exact tactical maneuvers when dribbling.

- Keep the ball in tight and close to your foot; do not let it roll off.
- Guide the ball at first with your strong foot but change soon to your weaker one. That way you will not be so predictable.
- Always have your body positioned between the ball and your opponent. This allows you to shield the ball, keeping it safe from an opponent's attempt at interference.
- Once you have become more confident, you can briefly take your eyes off the ball to take in the progress of the game and know where to play the ball after dribbling.
- Couple dribbling with feints and dummies.
- Dribble fast and have the guts to take risks. Especially if you are in the opponent's half. Refrain from dribbling near your own goal, this is much too dangerous.
- Once you have successfully dummied round an opponent, quickly finish off your dribbling with a pass to a teammate or a shot at goal.
- Do not overdo your dribbling, otherwise you will end up losing the ball too often and your teammates will be doing a lot of running around for nothing.

Training for your dribbling

 Practice controlling the ball without opponents

Zigzag runs out in the open (approx. 50 ft from one line to the next and then back)

Guide the ball ahead with the inside of your foot in a diagonal zigzag direction
• *one touch right, one left*
• *two touches right, two left*
• *three touches right, three left*

Guide the ball ahead with the inside and outside of your foot alternately in a zigzag direction
• *one touch right inside, followed by one touch right outside*
• *one touch left inside, followed by one touch left outside*
• *one touch right inside, followed by one touch left outside and then vice-versa, left inside and right outside*

Guide the ball ahead with only the outside of your foot alternately in a zigzag direction
• one touch right outside, then circle round the ball (important, otherwise you will not be able to play the ball with the next outside!), then one touch left outside
• two touches right outside, circle round the ball, then two touches left outside

Roll the ball along with the sole and the outside of your foot alternately in a zigzag direction
• one touch left sole, followed by one touch right outside
• one touch right sole, followed by one touch left outside
• one touch right inside, followed by one touch left sole, and then vice-versa, left inside and right sole

Come up with your own patterns at home or together with your coach.

Dribbling exercises with a passive opponent

Running through cones

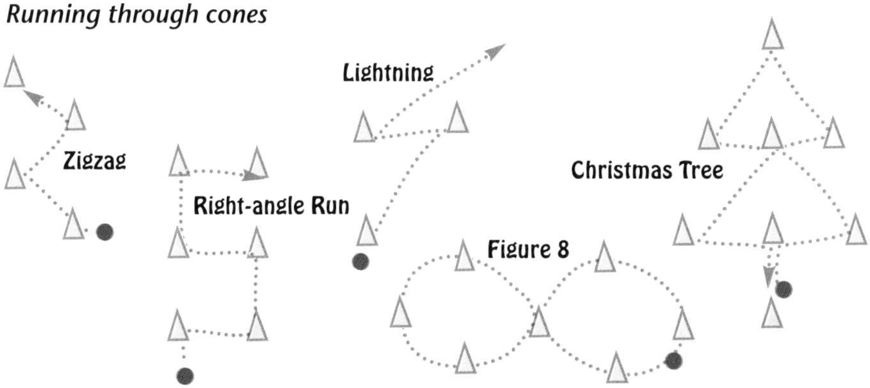

Lightning

Zigzag

Right-angle Run

Christmas Tree

Figure 8

Guide the ball from one cone to the next, continually changing the foot you use to dribble the ball. Come up with your own figures.

- Clip the ball solely with the inside of your foot.
- Clip the ball solely with the outside of your foot.
- Turn in just before the cone and clip the ball with the inside of your foot so that it remains shielded from the cone (which will later be an opponent), then continue on to the next cone and turn in the opposite direction.
- Using just your right or just your left foot, clip the ball from one cone to the next (you will notice that you will have to alternate between the inside and the outside of the same foot).

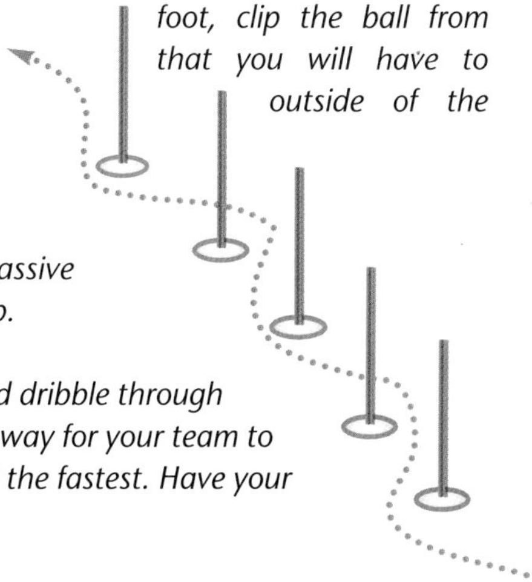

Slalom course

Dribble the ball through slalom poles (passive opponents) and try not to get caught up.

Position the poles about 5 feet apart and dribble through them as fast as you can. This is an easy way for your team to determine who can dribble the best and the fastest. Have your coach time you with his stopwatch.

Paced dribbling

The cones are placed down completely at random spots. As you dribble around them, clip the ball with the inside or outside of your foot right before you sidestep the pole.

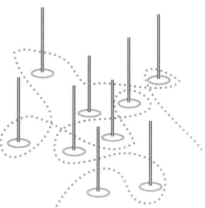

Dribbling the pole jungle

The poles are positioned close together (3-6 ft). Five or six players all dribble their balls through the pole jungle without touching another player or losing their ball.

Combine dribbling with dummy maneuvers (drawing back, kick feints, stride feints, scissoring, step-overs).

Combine dribbling with follow-up actions (passing and shooting).

 Dribbling exercises against a semi-active opponent

All the exercises you can do with a passive opponent, meaning poles, cones, etc., you can also include in your training sessions one or more real opponents. When you do these kinds of exercises, you are only being "semi-actively" attacked, meaning not the degree you would be in an actual match situation. Nor is it an all-out fight for the ball in this case, you are treated with more of a "hands-off" policy.

The main thing here is that you become familiar with and can practice your dribbling reaction on an opponent, both from a space and timing aspect, just as you would in a match.

Once you have successfully played round an opponent, he lets you run free. He is only on the offensive up to a certain point or within a certain zone.

Dribbling exercises/play against an active opponent

You can also do all these training exercises together with one or more active-ly-engaged opponents. They will be attacking, reacting and fighting for possession of the ball to the same extent as in an actual match.

It is best to practice all the game formations your coach picks for you, so you can consciously use and hone your dribbling in a real match-like situation. And this is also something easily practiced at home with your friends.

4-on-4 game (or 3-on-3) without goals, crossing lines
A "goal" has been scored when a player dribbles the ball across the opponent's line.

Short-sided games
Play 5 against 3 or 6 against 4 with two or more goals; dribbling is easier for the team having more players.

Multi-goal games
4-on-4 or 5-on-5 where a goal is scored only when a player dribbles the ball past a flag goal (3-6 ft wide) and can then pass the ball to another teammate.

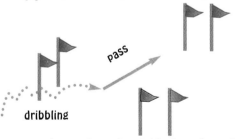

pass

dribbling

As you now know, learning technique is a step-by-step process. You start at the easiest level and progress up to the hardest. When you are first learning a new technique, choose exercises which are not so hard at the beginning and only then gradually increase the degree of difficulty as you go along.

Ball trapping and taking the ball on

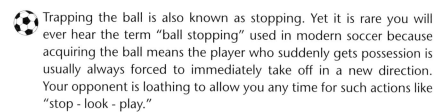 Trapping the ball is also known as stopping. Yet it is rare you will ever hear the term "ball stopping" used in modern soccer because acquiring the ball means the player who suddenly gets possession is usually always forced to immediately take off in a new direction. Your opponent is loathing to allow you any time for such actions like "stop - look - play."

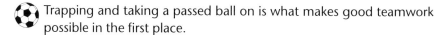 Trapping and taking a passed ball on is what makes good teamwork possible in the first place.

 Ball control is an important "tool" of a soccer player.

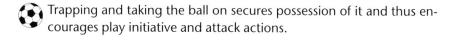 Trapping and taking the ball on secures possession of it and thus encourages play initiative and attack actions.

How is a ball trapped?

With all parts of both feet
- inside of the foot
- inner instep
- outside of the foot
- full instep
- sole

With other parts of the body
- head
- chest
- thigh

Techniques for trapping and taking the ball on depend on:

- the angle of the approaching ball (sharp, smooth)
- the trajectory (shallow, semi-high, high)
- the distance of the approaching ball (far, near)
- the time and the space available to a player to get the ball under control
- the position of an opponent and the type of threat he poses

Trapping and controlling shallow balls

The most important trapping technique is the trapping and controlling of the ball with the inside of the foot. This is the safest and also the most quickly learned type of ball control. But all other sides and areas of the foot can also be just as adept at trapping and controlling a ball.

Trapping and control of high (bouncing and flying) balls

Here the body part which will touch the ball first (head, thigh, inside of foot or instep) turns a little to meet the ball. After contact, the ball is smoothly slipped ("plucked") downward to land precisely in front of both feet and then immediately played on.

The smooth downward and rear-ward cushioning of the ball by the head, the thigh, the inside of the foot or the instep is important to ensure that the ball lands softly at your feet. If this is not done, the ball will bounce off – easy pickings for your opponents.

Just after trapping the ball, you have to move it along in another direction so you can shake off the opponent's attack.

Try to get control of bouncing and flying balls as quickly as possible and then get the ball flat on the ground again in front of your feet ready to play on. This will not only help in keeping the game going, but teamwork will benefit as well.

Practice tips

1. Trapping and taking the ball on from a stationary position, moving forward into the direction from which the ball was played.

2. Trapping and taking the ball on while in motion and running in the direction from which the ball was played.

3. Trapping and taking the ball on while in motion and turning to the side or backward into another direction than from where the ball was played to you.

4. Trapping and taking the ball on combined with other exercises
e.g. passing – taking the ball on sideways – dribbling – driving/cross pass.

As you can see from this series of steps, trapping is also a learned skill – starting with the easiest and gradually progressing on up to the hardest.

flying balls, sideways
flying balls, frontal
bouncing balls, sideways
bouncing balls, frontal
rolling balls, sideways
rolling balls, frontal

Tactical tips for trapping and taking the ball on

● Combine trapping with body feints, like drawing back motions or side stepping feints, conceal your intentions from your opponent.

● Always keep the ball in play in the new direction of movement. This will let you take action faster.

● Shield the ball from a threatening opponent. Place your body between the ball and the opponent.

● Run towards the ball because your opponent is – just like you are – always ready to put up a fight for it.

● Calculate approaching flying and bouncing balls correctly. Judge the distance and the angle and do not react too early or too late. If at all possible, let the ball bounce once in front of you, otherwise your opponent may very well turn out to be its "mocking" possessor.

● After first touch, think immediately ahead to the next course of action – either passing on to another teammate or going for a goal.

Tackling

The objective of tackling is to separate the opponent from the ball, to take the ball away from him or her and, as a logical consequence, to get control of it for yourself and your team.

Particularly in youth training, heavy emphasis is placed on making goals, while preventing goals often receives far less attention. Yet the game consists equally of actions and situations we can classify as:

- *attack and defend*
- *ball possession and ball loss*

The smallest unit of such actions when fighting for the ball is the *one-on-one*. Numerous statistics and clever coach analyses never cease to confirm:

The side which wins the most one-on-one showdowns wins the game!

Success in one-on-one contests chiefly has to do with ball possession. Only the player who is in possession of the ball can score goals and attack opponents. Looking at it from the other side of the coin, when your team does not have possession of the ball, you have to take the offensive in getting it back as quickly as possible, stealing it away from your opponent, and preventing your opponent from attacking and scoring.

Player prerequisites for successful tackling

- courage and determination in fighting the opponent with all fair means
- relentlessness in one-on-one contests, standing up to the tenacity of the opponent in possession of the ball
- finesse and skill in fighting for the ball
- actions based on skillful tactics (marking, positional play, anticipating moves) in order to deal with as few one-on-one contests as possible and to get possession of the ball beforehand
- good, defensive techniques focused on the ball

Technically, defensive technique is also referred to as "tackling."

Defense techniques

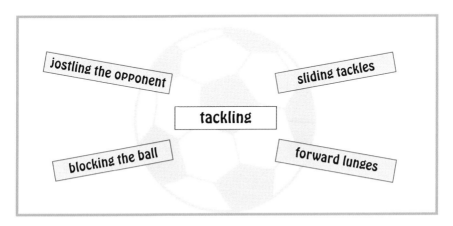

jostling the opponent

sliding tackles

tackling

blocking the ball

forward lunges

What in the world is that?

Only the best idea I have ever had, Coach! Now I am guaranteed to trap every ball!

Jostling the opponent

Two players are side by side. The player in defense tries to nudge his opponent away with the force of his shoulder so that he will become separated from the ball.

Even if the player cannot separate the other guy from the ball completely, he can always try to send the ball over the sideline or "toe it" off to a teammate, thereby destroying the opponent's attacking action.

Jostling must never escalate into knocking your opponent down. It is likewise prohibited to charge from behind or use your chest.

How to practice:

- Two players bump shoulders from the front and from the side while stationary.
- While running, jostle your partner with the upper part of your arms touching at the same height (no ball involved).
- Jostle a dribbling partner with your upper arm and shoulder.
- Jostle a dribbling partner with your upper arm and shoulder while trying to toe the ball away from him.
- 1-on-1 contest with mini-goals for just 30 seconds, then change partners. Remember to take breaks.

Blocking the ball

The player in possession of the ball is separated from it by you blocking the ball from the front with the inside of your foot. The foot of your kicking leg has to be angled here just like an inside-of-the-foot kick, both your legs are bent at the knee and your ankle held rigid. All your leg muscles are tensed in preparation for any shot made by the opponent.

The foot is held tightly against the ball. The object is to block the opponent such that the ball ends up being squeezed up over his foot.

 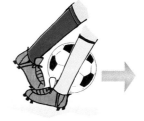

The defensive player should not kick at the ball energetically, because in this type of blocking play, it is usually the player making the first move who loses the ball.

How to practice:

- Block the ball from the front with the sole of your foot while stationary. Both partners block simultaneously. Who has the better technique and the greater strength?
- Block the ball with the inside of your foot while your opponent dribbles.
- Block the ball with the inside of your foot while executing a fall. The attack on the opponent comes from the side and the blocking leg is bent.
- 1-on-1 contest with mini-goals for just 30 seconds, then change partners. Remember to take breaks.

Sliding tackles

Here the player in defense attempts to toe the ball away from the attacker's foot by sliding in sideways. In so doing, he angles the sliding foot so that he can hook the ball away and play on.

The support leg is bent at the knee and positioned well behind, as if about to hurdle. The kicking leg is stretched out and slides along the ground to the ball. With his upper body slanting away from the opponent, the player falls, both arms stretched outwardly to the side to break his fall.

Sliding tackles are risky, because it is not always clearly recognizable whether only the ball was actually played (permissible) or whether the opponent's leg was also hit (against the rules). It means walking a fine line at the edge of being sent off or being shown a yellow card.

How to practice:

- Falling exercises without ball or opponent
- Sliding toward a ball without opponents
- Sliding tackles at a ball rolling away, without opponents
- Sliding tackles with a run-up to a stationary ball and passive opponent
- Sliding tackles against a dribbling, semi-active opponent who consciously keeps the ball far forward
- Sliding tackles against an active swiftly-dribbling opponent
- One-on-one contests into mini-goals

Note that only those who are very confident with this defensive technique should actually use it. After all, a main consideration when playing is the health and well-being of all players, as is the playing of a fair game. Respect for your opponent is the supreme commandment in soccer.

One should also be really sure about this move because the defensive player can miss the ball when coming in with a slide and then he lands up on the ground. The opponent, remaining in possession of the ball, may now conceivably break away, making it a breeze for him or her to continue the attack or go for a goal.

Forward lunges

Bursting out in front of an opponent at an angle from behind to intercept a pass to another opponent. The ball is brought under control using the inside of the kicking leg's foot or played on in order to defuse an opponent's goal-threatening action. Once you have secured the ball, you can start a new attack yourself.

What is important to keep in mind with these lunges is getting your body between the ball and the opponent. The opponent cannot see the rapid

approach coming up from behind. Use this element of surprise to your advantage. If your lunge does not pan out because you surface too late and the opponent remains in control of the ball, call up another defensive technique. The main thing is to prevent your opponent from advancing on the goal with the ball.

How to practice:

- Reaction exercise in lunging forward on a passive opponent without a ball. The signal comes from the coach as a shout or whistle.
- Lunge forward against a passive opponent moving forwards or to the side with the ball after receiving it directly in front of him.
- Lunge forward against an active opponent with play carrying depending on who gets possession of the ball.
- 3:2 to 4:3 short-sided games for mini-goals with conscious use of forward lunges. The team with the lesser number of players attempts to come into possession of the ball faster or even at all.

Tactical tips for the defense

Whenever possible, always try to thwart your opponent
before or at least during trapping; after he has the ball,
it will always be much harder.

•

Always keep an eye on the opponent and the ball.
Pay attention to how the game is progressing.

•

Cover the inside line, meaning always drive the opponent away
to the outside, toward the sideline.
Prevent him running inside you towards the goal.

•

After you get possession of the ball, immediately pass to
an unmarked teammate or into an open space.
You can also dribble out of the danger zone.

•

Upon losing the ball, immediately switch to defense to win it back.

•

The nearer to the goal, the tighter you have to mark the opponent.

•

Never play the ball crossways through the penalty area,
but always away from the goal.

•

Delay an opponent coming toward you as long as possible, until your
teammates have the chance to run up and help you (delaying defense).

•

Never make the first move, wait for your opponent's action
and concentrate on the ball.

•

Keep your own moves lightning-fast and decisive, but fair.

The header

Playing the ball with the head is a unique – and at times a spectacular – way to pass the ball through the air.

Possible use of headers

 Playing a high incoming ball on to a teammate
Example: The goalie kicks the ball and the center forward sends it on to his winger with a header

 Precision header at goal with intent to score
Example: Cross pass in the penalty area and a precisely-placed header into the net

 Defending by heading incoming balls to prevent opponent attack at goal
Example: Cross pass in the goal area and defender's header sends the ball out of the danger zone

Types of headers

- from a stationary position (legs apart)
- from a jump (one or two-leg jump)
- diving header (one or two-leg jump)

Since headers are usually done while jumping, this type of jump requires a special technique:

- Jump with both or just one leg (the jumping leg for right-handers is often the left leg)
- Forcefully hurl arms and jumping leg upward
- Jump for height, not distance
- Always try to land on both feet

Things to remember with headers

- The ball is hit with the forehead (ideally hitting the ball dead center)
- Neck is stiff
- Chin pulled inward and down toward the chest
- Eyes are open
- Body is coiled (upper body arches from the hips)
- Quick forward thrust of upper body and forceful follow-through with the entire body

There are also mistakes you should avoid. Use a pencil to check off any problems you might still be struggling with.

☐ The jump is not high enough yet, instead more of a forward direction.

☐ Poor judging of the incoming ball. Jumping too early or too late.

☐ Header not hit with the forehead but with the top of the head. This will send the ball flying off upward.

If you are having trouble with headers, figure out exactly what the problem is and discuss it with your coach so the two of you can come up with suitable training exercises.

Practice suggestions

- Practice "dry runs" of the motions.
- First practice the header without a ball.
- Have your coach throw you well-placed balls at eye level. Start from a stationary position.
- Practice juggling the ball with your head so that you will get the feel for doing headers with your forehead.
- Practice balancing the ball on your forehead.

Simple exercises for mastering headers:

- If you are practicing alone, head the ball against a wall. When you are practicing together with a friend or partner, head the ball back and forth to one another through the air.

- Set up two identical goals roughly 15 feet apart. One of you throws the ball high up into the air, the other tries to score only by means of headers.

- Header distance competition
  Who can head the ball the farthest after throwing himself up a ball?

Now getting more difficult:

Hand – Head – Ball – Play
Play handball on half a regulation pitch. Scoring is only allowed by headers. This means that passes must be precisely timed to come in at head height so that the player heading the ball can make good use of it.

Diving headers for the courageous
Practice diving headers on a soft surface. Your partner plays the ball to you shallow and sharp. Jump bravely and parallel to the ground with one leg, pull your head back into your neck, eyes open, and "sail" into the oncoming ball, heading it sharply back. All you need for this exercise is a measure of courage and the oldest clothes you have got!

Using your head on corner kicks
All the players of a team – both attackers as well as defensive players –position themselves in the penalty area. The coach or other players hit high balls as cross passes into the goal area from both respective outer positions. The defending players try to head the balls away from the area while the attackers try to score with headers. The goalkeeper can intervene; he can fist the ball off, catch it and run out.

Which side is better? The defense or the attack?

Practicing with a pendulum header unit

Many soccer clubs now have pendulum header units. Such a unit consists of a tall mast with a ball suspended from a rope. Since this resourceful device rebounds balls right back at you after you have struck them, it lets you get in some very good header training, whether you are alone or being instructed from the sidelines.

What can one learn and train on the pendulum?

- *how to properly judge a ball's trajectory (distancing)*
- *the proper run-up and jump to meet a ball*
- *the proper way to land*
- *the right way to meet the ball with your forehead (the ball never comes in from above, always from the front!)*
- *how to coil your body*
- *keeping your eyes open during headers (no fear since there is no opponent!)*

Practice ideas

 Headers following a two-leg jump

The player stands in front of the pendulum unit and uses both legs to jump up. He heads the ball with just a quick tap of his forehead (the ball should not swing off too far, not more than two feet). As soon as the player lands back down on the ground, he jumps up forcefully again to head the ball as it returns (do 5-6 headers, one right after the other). The pendulum unit should not be adjusted too high for this exercise. When you are standing under it, there should be just about a half an inch of room between your head and the ball.

This exercise helps you become accustomed to the pendulum-like motion of the ball and learn to perform the proper technical sequence.

　　　(forehead – coiled body– eyes open – neck stiff)

Headers following a two-leg jump after a run-up

The player stands 3-10 feet in front of the pendulum unit and then runs up to it, ideally in a triple run-up rhythm like in basketball (left-right-left). He then pushes upward with both legs. He heads the ball off upward and forward with a solid impact from his forehead. The ball will now pivot away. Once the player lands, he runs behind and waits for the ball to reach the highest point in its pendulum motion from him. When the ball reaches the point where it changes direction and starts to swing back to the player, he runs back up to it and tries to head it perfectly so it will bound off far away again. The pendulum unit must be set somewhat higher for this exercise.

This exercise helps train headers used in defense and for attacks following corner and free kicks. These balls have a long, calculable trajectory and there is no opportunity or room for a lengthy run-up.

Headers following a one-leg jump after a run-up

The player stands 3-10 feet away from the pendulum unit and runs up to it aggressively. He jumps up with one leg forward, heading the ball off upward and forward with his forehead.

This exercise helps train both defensive and offensive headers following cross kicks, throw-ins, corner and free kicks. It is also well-suited for dealing with balls which come flying in rapidly, meaning you need a forceful and fast run-up.

Variations:
- *Another player can also head the returning ball.*
- *Twist your body before making the header so that the ball is then sent off to the side.*

No pendulum header unit available? Then build your own! Wrap a ball up in a ball net and hang it by a cord from the crossbeam, a clothesline or a tree branch.

Feints

Playing round an opponent is also a skill that is learned. A player can only run past an opponent keeping the ball at his feet if he is faster than his opponent or manages to outwit him. You can move your body in ways to trick him into going in the opposite or a different direction, thereby creating space for yourself to run past him. That is exactly what the whole idea and purpose behind a feint is!

Yet, as you can easily imagine, your opponent will not simply step aside and politely let you perform such trickery to get round him. He is striving to get the ball back onto his own side, so he is certainly not going to meekly let you pass it without putting up a fight. He will be using the best of his own defensive technique to win it back. The more skillful you are, the easier it will be for you to play round an opponent.

You have to mask your intentions, deceive your opponent, and use every (fair) trick in the book to get away with this!

What does successfully deceiving an opponent in soccer mean?

- You have passed him (left him behind), got closer to the goal and thus, given an open opportunity, can shoot at goal without distraction, interference or any threat.

- You create a short-sided state in your team's favor. You have now one player more in play, meaning you can pass to an open, unmarked teammate. This increases your threat of scoring a goal.

- You chip away at your opponent's self-confidence because he falls for your tricks and body deceptions and cannot get to the ball. This annoys him and, in turn, he grows weaker.

- Selling dummies and feinting lets you avoid one-on-one contests, keeps you from getting injured, and allows you to continue your action after playing through with either a shot at goal, passing to a teammate or dribbling onward.

What different kinds of feints are there?

Body feints   Tricking your opponent by moving your body a certain way.

Ball feints   Tricking your opponent by moving the ball a certain way.

Glance feints Tricking your opponent by where you look (looking right, playing left)

Vocal feints   Tricking your opponent by fake calls (calling to one teammate, playing to another)

Important body feints

The side-step feint

Lead the ball toward your opponent with your right foot. Just before you meet, make a wide lunge with your right foot to the right. Your opponent will match this movement (think of him as now being on the wrong foot) while you suddenly play past him with the ball at your feet on the left.

Important: Act fast! When your opponent makes the wrong move, play the ball quickly past him with the outside of your left foot, if you are getting by him on the left, and then immediately increase the distance between the two of you.

The side-step feint is, of course, also possible to the right. Once you have got good at it, try a double side-step feint. For example: feint to the right, then to the left, and only after that do you take the ball off in the first direction.

The scissors

Lead the ball toward your opponent with your strong foot. Just before you meet (approx. one yard apart), execute a scissors-like motion around the ball with your right foot, from the right outside to the left inside. Scissor motion means that you cross your legs, literally "scissor" them, while the ball rolls on between your crossed legs. After the scissor motion, set your right foot next to the ball on the left and then lead the ball on in the other direction with your outer right instep. Your opponent will match this movement to the left (remember, he is on the wrong foot) while you run past him with the ball at your feet.

Of course you can also do the scissors feint with the other leg toward the other side. Try the double scissors, too! Start the scissors on the right without contact to the ball, then immediately scissor your left leg around the ball and only then do you pick up the ball again with the outer instep or with the inside of your free, unobstructed foot.

The Okocha feint

(named after J. J. Okocha, a player of the Nigeria national team)

Run towards the ball lying in front of you. With one foot, take a step over the ball and then clamp it between your feet (heel of the front foot and instep of the rear foot). You now tilt your entire body forward, especially your upper torso. In doing so, you pop the ball up into the air and release it so it will fly forward in an arch over your head or your shoulder.

Important: *Raise your heel or the inside of your lower foot so that a flying momentum is given to the ball from that point.*

Steps to learning the various different feints

Play tag/catching games in training sessions.
This teaches you deceptive and evading moves.

Also play ball games in which you can use your hands
like netball or basketball in your training sessions.
These games help you to learn and apply body feints more easily.

Practice performing feints step by step all alone without opponents.
Commit each movement to memory. Start off practicing with your strong
foot, meaning your strong foot carries out the feinting movement.

Set up some sort of obstruction to represent an opponent (a tree on a
field, a clothesline in the yard, a cone) and practice your feinting
sequence on it. This "opponent" is passive, meaning he will not
be trying anything and he will not be taking off with the ball.
This exercise helps teach you the spatial contingencies to feinting,
meaning how you have to calculate and carry out your moves so not to
be too close, but also not too far away from your opponent.

Practice feinting to the other side now, too; i.e., with your weak leg.
Your "opponent" remains passive.

Now move up to practicing against a "human opponent",
yet one who remains passive in that he matches
and allows your sideward feinting motions. You are still practicing your
execution, gaining a clear picture about how to start and follow
through with your feints. Then pick up the pace and move faster.

Now we get down to business – your opponent will actively react like he
would in an actual match and he will be trying to get the ball away from
you. It is all your decision now as to the side to which you will feint
(which the opponent will not know) and therefore
you now have the advantage. Use it!

Keep practicing continually faster and more aggressively. Your coach will
choose play formations (1:1, 2:2) so that you can play against one
another with a lot of ball contact and have every opportunity to run
through your different feints.

Some tactical tips for feinting

 Not too early, not too late
Choose the right moment in time, relative to your opponent's actions, otherwise he will not fall for your tricks.

 Not too far, not too close
Choose the right distance (roughly 4-6 feet), relative to your opponent's actions, otherwise his movements will not match your feint.

Change of pace
Before the feint, your pace reflects that of your opponent's actions and position. After the feint, pick up your pace to lightning speed, otherwise your opponent will catch you up again in the ensuing duel race.

Change of direction
Always combine a feint with a change of direction into an open space (from left to right, from behind to ahead, etc.). Otherwise you will have the next opponent right in front or next to you.

Once you become a master at feinting, you become an unpredictable force to be reckoned with and a great threat to your opponents. Practice your feinting over and over again during your practice sessions. Use one or two feints during an actual game. Concentrate on your favorite ones.

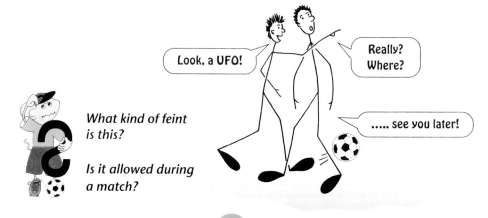

What kind of feint is this?

Is it allowed during a match?

Look, a UFO!

Really? Where?

..... see you later!

Training set play situations

Just as the elements of soccer technique should be practiced over and over again in your training sessions, tactical elements also need to be practiced repeatedly. You can play through entire game situations during training, each player knows the overall game plan as well as his own tasks and duties within it. These prepared and drilled game situations are referred to as set play situations.

The free kick

There are many different ways to shoot free kicks. Soccer rules distinguish between *direct* and *indirect* free kicks.

The direct free kick

The direct free kick can be made right into the goal by one player without any other player needing to touch the ball first. The kick counts as a goal if the ball goes over the opposing goal line. Free kicks can be made from different positions and distances from the goal or from right inside the box itself.

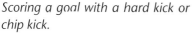

Scoring a goal with a hard kick or chip kick.

One of your teammates can also position himself in the wall and then bend over at just the right moment to let the ball through.

Or you chip the ball carefully over the wall. At the same moment, your teammate runs behind the wall, secures the ball and shoots the goal.

Free kicks are also made from the left and the right of the penalty area, from wing positions and from the midfield.

The indirect free kick

The indirect free kick can only be shot into the goal indirectly, meaning it first has to be touched by another player. The kick counts as a goal if the ball goes over the opposing goal line after having been touched.

Touching by another player includes:

- quick pass to another teammate who then shoots at goal
- passing to an open stationary or running teammate who can then directly convert the play
- kicking a long high ball into the penalty area and from there a header or kick at goal is made
- deliberately making a hard and direct free kick, gambling on the opponent or one's own side deflecting the ball into the net (if no one manages to touch the ball, the goalkeeper can simply let it through, the goal will not count!)

Three players ready for a free kick. Two of them run off, feint kicking the ball while actually running past it. The third player makes the free kick and passes it to one of the other two. This second player then goes for the goal.

Use this drawing to sketch in other variants!

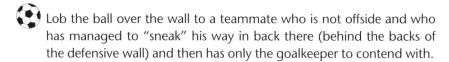 Lob the ball over the wall to a teammate who is not offside and who has managed to "sneak" his way in back there (behind the backs of the defensive wall) and then has only the goalkeeper to contend with.

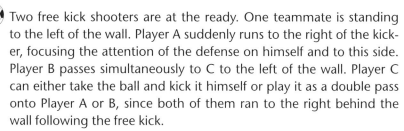 Two free kick shooters are at the ready. One teammate is standing to the left of the wall. Player A suddenly runs to the right of the kicker, focusing the attention of the defense on himself and to this side. Player B passes simultaneously to C to the left of the wall. Player C can either take the ball and kick it himself or play it as a double pass onto Player A or B, since both of them ran to the right behind the wall following the free kick.

The three players need to master precise passing and quick handling. You should first practice this play in training, totally concentrated, over and over again. Better still, rehearse and drill it into your heads, so that you can synchronize each other's movements and actions during a match.

The corner kick

It is not without good reason that soccer reporters keep track of corner kick ratios in addition to goals. While they may not tell us anything about the final score, they do indicate which team can be the more deadly in scoring goals. In addition, a corner kick always offers a superb chance of scoring. As the saying goes, "He converted a corner!" It is up to the players to exploit this scoring opportunity for all it is worth. Those who have faithfully practiced the set play situations during training are now at an advantage.

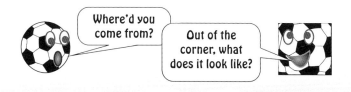

Three variations of the corner kick

 Long corner kick into the penalty area
The ball is kicked in as a long high ball towards the far post or at least level with the penalty spot.

There are two ways to play it.

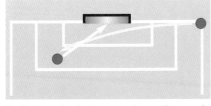 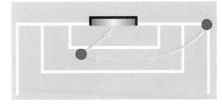

1. *Swing the ball away from the goal. From the right corner, a right-legged kicker has to kick the shot; a left-legged kicker from the left corner.*

2. *Swing the ball towards the goal. From the right corner, a left-legged kicker then has to kick the shot; a right-legged kicker from the left corner.*

 Short corner kick
The ball is sent to the rear area to another player. He or she runs up from the midfield, and, depending upon the opponent's defensive actions, plays this corner kick as a cross pass, semi-high drive, or passes it back into the goal area.

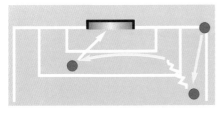 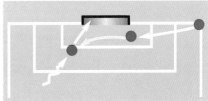

 Short corner kick along the sideline
The ball is played high to the near post (closest to the corner). A player is already in position there, sending the ball on with a header back toward the far post. Another teammate shoots for the goal using either his head or his foot.

The throw-in

This manner of getting a soccer ball in motion with one's hands is a relic from the game's earliest beginnings, back when the game was still a mixture of hand and foot technique (now today's rugby).

At what point is a ball thrown in?

When a ball is kicked or goes over a sideline, the other team receives a throw-in at the exact spot where the ball crossed the line.

This is the only time a fielder can play the ball with his hands. The player must be behind the sideline outside the playing field and not cross over the line. To give the ball momentum, it is held between both hands and behind the head, the actual throw itself also uses both hands. Both feet remain on the ground.

Anything else is an illegal throw-in and the referee will penalize for it. Some players, attempting to buy themselves a few feet, will try to get the throw-in to another spot nearer the other half. A quick run-up during your throw is allowed, provided you stop at the line.

Hey, Billy! You call that a throw-in? Or do you think you are playing marbles here?

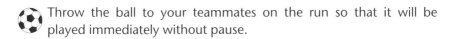

Tactical tips and hints for the throw-in

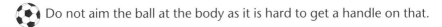 Throw the ball to your teammates on the run so that it will be played immediately without pause.

Do not aim the ball at the body as it is hard to get a handle on that.

Those who can throw a ball a good distance should "catapult" it sharply toward the goal, like a strong cross pass into the penalty area (with run-up, great backward momentum, coiled body).

When the throw-in comes bouncing or flying up high to you, maneuver your body between the ball and your opponent while shielding the ball and trapping it with your thigh or chest, then quickly hook it down to rest on the ground so that you can then continue the play with your feet again.

Do not aim the throw-in straight down the line, which is where the majority of your opponents are just waiting for a nice little round present! It is better to throw the ball to a teammate on the field who can get a handle on it without immediately losing it again or letting it go out over the sideline.

Note: the offside rule is suspended during a throw-in, meaning a player cannot be offside during a throw-in and you can then take your opponent by surprise with a swift throw.

Look over at the left page. Why is Billy's throw-in all wrong? What decision does the referee award for an illegal throw-in?

During a match, you must always have an overview of the whole game. Part of this demands that you can assess or "read" the overall game situation and then make the right decision on how to act. And all of that in a split second. Players communicate with one another by means of looks or shouts. Many situations are practiced in training and each player knows what is expected of him.

Besides actual training on a soccer field, practice can also be drilled in theory by means of sketches prior to a game.

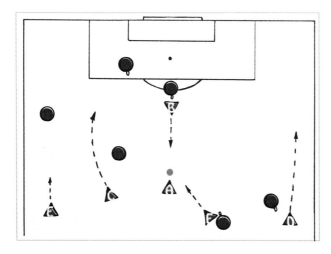

1. 'Call' for the ball (by moving in)

2. 'Call' for the ball (by retreating quickly)

3. Dash away/off

4. Run across

5. Run alongside

 Player A is in possession of the ball. What options for running on to the ball do his teammates B, C, D, E and F have? Write the corresponding numbers on the dotted lines.

 What play can the player in possession of the ball execute to his unmarked teammates? Add arrows to the sketch for the direction of play.

Which basic rules for running on to the ball can you jot down? To help you, We have provided a number of questions.

Why should you run on to the ball?

When should you run on to the ball?

How should you run on to the ball?

Where should you run to get on the ball?

You are the player in the sketch depicted by the triangle. Sketch how you can successfully follow dribbling with a shot at goal.

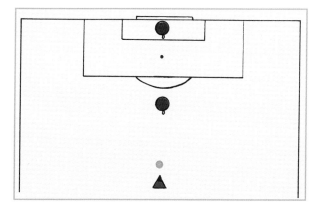

Have you ever wondered what a referee would do if something totally unexpected or bizarre happened during a match?

We have noted some of these types of unusual events on the next two pages. Check the answer you think is right!

WHAT HAPPENS WHEN ....?

 What happens when a spectator runs onto the field and scores a goal?

A The goal counts.

B The goal does not count. The referee stops the game and then continues it with a dropped ball.

C The goal does not count since the spectator is not wearing a jersey from the team he just made the goal for.

 What happens when a dog runs onto the field and chews up the ball?

A The ball is quickly mended as best as possible and the dog chained up together with its owner.

B The referee blows the final whistle. Whatever the score is at that point becomes the final score.

C The referee stops the game, replaces the damaged ball with a new one, and then continues the game with a dropped ball.

 What happens when a throw-in lands in the opposing goal?

A The goal counts.

B The goal only counts if the throw-in crosses the goal line in the air.

C The goal does not count because a player cannot score any goal with his hands. The game is continued with a goal kick.

 What happens when a penalty kick is scored only after a follow-up by the same player?

A The goal only counts if the goalkeeper fended off the ball beforehand.

B The goal does not count because the scorer played the ball twice.

C The goal only counts if the ball hit the goalpost beforehand.

What happens when a free kick is immediately played a second time by the same player?

A He is allowed to do so. If he scores a goal by doing so, it counts.

B This is not allowed. A ball at rest cannot be played twice in a row by the same player.

C He is allowed to do so but only and if he does not score a goal by doing so.

What happens when two players make a penalty kick?

A This is only possible when they tie their legs together at the knees with a belt (Player A's right leg to Player B's left leg).

B This is not possible because only one kicker is allowed.

C This is possible when the first player plays the ball forward into the penalty area and the second player, heeding the distance limits in the penalty area, runs in and shoots.

What happens when a player's corner kick is a direct score?

A This is possible and a valid goal.

B This is not possible because a player cannot score any direct goal from the corner.

C This is only possible if the corner kicker had previously informed the referee and loudly announces his intended goal before going for it.

What happens when a player wears two different colored shoes?

A This is not possible because an opponent could mix up the colors and, in his uncertainty, always plays the ball to this particular player.

B This is only possible if the player has previously got in touch with both shoe manufacturers and asked their permission.

C This is allowed and left up to each player's individual sense of style and fashion.

.....10 HEALTHY THROUGH AND THROUGH

Those who believe that strenuous and sweaty training a couple of times a week is sufficient to ensure athletic prowess all on its own, will no doubt quickly be set straight. Besides all the physical training you need, phases during which you can rest and recuperate are also very important, as is getting enough sleep, ensuring a healthy diet, body hygiene, an orderly life and much, much more.

You should learn to recognize and listen to your "inner clock". It is what regulates your biological rhythms and it will let you know when you are particularly raring to go, compared to when you desperately need a little R&R and would be better off just taking it easy for a while. As another example, a good soccer player can also sense when he needs high-energy food in order to remain at peak power and fully concentrated.

This chapter delves into some interesting information on this topic. Take this as a suggestion to get more involved with your own body, your own "inner clock" and a healthier diet. Have fun!

mid-morning   afternoon

noon

morning

night

Physical efficiency and capability

As the above curve shows you, our productivity experiences various highs and lows over the course of a full day. All of us go through such peaks and troughs and we all adjust our daily life to this seesaw rhythm. Your primary focus, your classes at school, take place in the morning while sometimes by lunchtime you may even find yourself starting to nod off. After we get our "second wind" in the afternoon, our bodies are given their well-deserved sleep at night. If you take this rhythm into account, you will live a healthy life and be very productive. You can easily tell when you have not got enough rest or sleep, while not taking advantage of those great "highs" would be an awful shame.

Eat and drink yourself into shape!

Athletes who eat and drink too much or the wrong things before training or competition are not productive. They feel stuffed, tired and worn-out. Many of our bodily functions go into slow mode because the stomach has to work at top speed. But eating – and especially drinking – is something we all have to do in order to give our bodies the energy it needs and to compensate for the fluid we lose when we perspire. It is necessary (and important!) to pay attention to this – even in the middle of long training sessions or competitive matches.

Figure out a basic overview of what would be suitable for your main meals, for snacks between meals, and for those periodic spurts of energy. Make sure what you eat and drink, as well as the times you eat and drink, is sufficient to carry you through training and matches, but that you are not digesting your food at the same time either.

How long food remains in the stomach before being fully digested:

approx. 1 hour: *water, tea, broth*
approx. 2-3 hours: cocoa, banana, apple, roll, rice, cooked fish, soft-boiled egg, whole-grain bread, cake, buttered bread, granola, vegetables
approx. 4-5 hours: cold cuts, meat, fried potatoes, French fries, beans, peas
approx. 6-7 hours: cream cakes, mushrooms, fish in oil, fatty roasted foods

---

Pouring out sweat means pouring in liquids

In order to compensate for the fluid you lose by sweating, you need to drink a lot of liquids during training and matches. Otherwise your productivity will dwindle, your blood will "thicken", because it is not able to take in as much oxygen, and you may very well end up with muscle cramps.

 Suitable drinks before and during exertion
mineral water, fruit juice mixed with soda water at a concentration of about 1:3, lightly sweetened drinks

 Suitable drinks after exertion
fruit juice mixed with soda water, the fruit juice now at a higher concentration, milk drinks, drinks with a higher sugar content

This food pyramid shows which foods you should consume in large quantities (bottom) and which foods are better to enjoy only on very rare occasions (top).

Examples are given for each of these various food groups.

cake,
hard and
soft candies
chocolate bars,

milk, cheese, yogurt,
cold cuts, meat, eggs,
beans, peas, nuts

banana, apple, orange, kiwi, carrot,
tomato, lettuce, broccoli, cucumber,

bread, potato, rice, pasta, granola, cornflakes

mineral water, fruit juice + soda water, tea

Find eleven different fruits and vegetables horizontally, vertically, diagonally or backwards

M	K	A	P	O	T	A	T	O	E	S	A	B	I	F
Z	U	C	C	H	I	N	I	D	N	J	R	Q	U	A
K	N	U	I	S	E	G	N	A	R	O	T	T	B	A
I	S	C	A	L	E	T	T	U	C	E	I	A	L	H
S	Q	U	A	S	H	O	K	C	G	R	A	P	E	S
K	A	M	T	H	L	E	O	E	R	N	Q	W	M	E
S	K	B	Y	E	J	L	A	S	A	O	N	P	O	H
G	H	E	R	P	I	N	E	A	P	P	L	E	N	C
C	A	R	R	O	T	S	J	O	E	H	N	P	S	A
V	E	S	R	M	P	O	N	T	F	S	R	P	P	N
S	E	I	R	R	E	B	W	A	R	T	S	E	X	I
S	A	N	A	N	A	B	C	E	U	L	I	R	A	P
L	C	L	I	Z	R	A	I	M	I	R	N	S	E	S
X	C	M	F	L	S	J	V	S	T	A	R	K	Z	J

.....10 Healthy Through and Through

Those who believe that strenuous and sweaty training a couple of times a week is sufficient to ensure athletic prowess all on its own, will no doubt quickly be set straight. Besides all the physical training you need, phases during which you can rest and recuperate are also very important, as is getting enough sleep, ensuring a healthy diet, body hygiene, an orderly life and much, much more.

You should learn to recognize and listen to your "inner clock". It is what regulates your biological rhythms and it will let you know when you are particularly raring to go, compared to when you desperately need a little R&R and would be better off just taking it easy for a while. As another example, a good soccer player can also sense when he needs high-energy food in order to remain at peak power and fully concentrated.

This chapter delves into some interesting information on this topic. Take this as a suggestion to get more involved with your own body, your own "inner clock" and a healthier diet. Have fun!

mid-morning

afternoon

noon

morning

night

Physical efficiency and capability

As the above curve shows you, our productivity experiences various highs and lows over the course of a full day. All of us go through such peaks and troughs and we all adjust our daily life to this seesaw rhythm. Your primary focus, your classes at school, take place in the morning while sometimes by lunchtime you may even find yourself starting to nod off. After we get our "second wind" in the afternoon, our bodies are given their well-deserved sleep at night. If you take this rhythm into account, you will live a healthy life and be very productive. You can easily tell when you have not got enough rest or sleep, while not taking advantage of those great "highs" would be an awful shame.

Eat and drink yourself into shape!

Athletes who eat and drink too much or the wrong things before training or competition are not productive. They feel stuffed, tired and worn-out. Many of our bodily functions go into slow mode because the stomach has to work at top speed. But eating – and especially drinking – is something we all have to do in order to give our bodies the energy it needs and to compensate for the fluid we lose when we perspire. It is necessary (and important!) to pay attention to this – even in the middle of long training sessions or competitive matches.

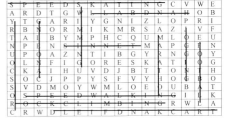

Page 12 Real Madrid (Spain), AC Milan (Italy), Ajax Amsterdam (Holland), Manchester United (England), FC Bayern Munich (Germany)

Page 15 Who we consider to be the world's best national teams:
Brazil (5-time World Cup champions, 7-time Copa America winners); Germany (3-time World Cup champions, 3-time European Cup champions); Italy (3-time World Cup champions, 1-time European Cup champions); Argentina (2-time World Cup champions, 14-time Copa America winners); France (1-time World Cup champions, 3-time European Cup champions)

Page 27 1. Tell your coach that your instep kick just is not working yet and you really want to concentrate on that for now.

2. Tell your coach that you have already got that down pat and you'd like to try practicing something a little more challenging.

Page 63 It is obvious that a team can only use fair, sportsmanlike means during a match. What the figure is relating here is total baloney!

Page 68

Page 84 Self-esteem – Having fun when playing – ~~Self-doubt~~ – ~~Blind rage~~ – Willingness to take risks – Laid-back approach – ~~Fear of making a mistake~~ – Ambition – Will to win – Confidence in your own performance – ~~Pessimism~~ – ~~Bad mood~~ – Feeling in good shape – Ability to concentrate

Page 90/91 *12-15 points*
With the attitude you bring to the sport, you will go far! You are having fun when playing and you can overcome your low moments as well. Keep it up!

8-11 points
While you have a good outlook on the game, sometimes you seem to be stuck in first gear. Have a little more fun with it and cultivate your will to win and you will be even more successful than ever!

5-7 points
You still need a little work on your attitude as far as fairness and camaraderie go. Take your training and your games seriously, be fair to your teammates and opponents, and have fun when playing!

Page 128 Of course, it is allowed! Any distracting of your opponent's attention from the ball is allowed. Outwitted with words and gestures! Poor baby!

Page 135 A correct throw is one done with both arms back over your head. The referee will call for an opponent throw-in at the exact same spot. (In the case of extremely young players whose arms just are not that long enough yet, a simpler throw-in can also be arranged prior to kicking off a game)

Page 136/137 This sketch shows the solution for Assignment 1 and 2:

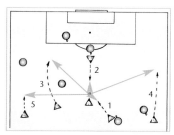

Assignment 3
- Creates play possibilities for teammates (triangular formation)
- The player running free determines the moment of passing
- To the ball, not behind your teammate and not on off ahead
- Into open space or toward the player in possession of the ball

Page 137

Page 144

M	K	A	P	O	T	A	T	O	E	S	A	B	I	F
Z	U	C	C	H	I	N	I	D	N	J	R	Q	U	A
K	N	U	I	S	E	G	N	A	R	O	T	T	B	A
I	S	C	A	L	E	T	T	U	C	E	I	A	L	H
S	Q	U	A	S	H	O	K	C	G	R	A	P	E	S
Y	I	M	T	I	I	I	E	Y	R	I	I	W	M	L
S	K	B	Y	E	J	L	A	S	A	O	N	P	O	H
G	H	E	R	P	I	N	E	A	P	P	L	E	N	C
C	A	R	R	O	T	S	J	O	E	H	N	P	S	A
V	E	S	R	M	P	O	N	T	F	S	R	P	P	N
S	E	I	R	R	E	B	W	A	R	T	S	E	X	I
S	A	N	A	N	A	B	C	E	U	L	I	R	A	P
L	C	L	I	Z	R	A	I	M	I	R	N	S	E	S
X	C	M	F	L	S	J	V	S	T	A	R	K	Z	J

Page 138/139 1 – B, 2 – C, 3 – C, 4 – A, 5 – B, 6 – C, 7 – A, 8 – C

12 THE GRAND FINALE

Dear soccer parents!

Becoming hooked on soccer does not take long. Soccer is today's fastest-growing sport, hands down. Your child decided to get into it too, and has already started practicing. Now he or she wants to stick with it, taking it even further by joining a club, training seriously, becoming part of a team. Do you know the reason why? Ask your child or let him or her show you the pages in this book concerning motivation. But one thing must be clear from the start: those who go into soccer training have the objective of success, of scoring goals and, together with their team, ultimate victory.

This training guide was written with young kickers in their first few years of training in mind. It provides them with a lot of information about their chosen sport, about the techniques and tactics involved, and just how important training is. They will learn how to recognize their own potential better and become more consciously aware of how to treat their bodies. This contributes not only to more effective training but also wards off both overtaxing as well as underachieving circumstances.

All players go through the same basic training and talent development, regardless of whether they will later view soccer as a leisure/weekend sport or whether they will move on to a leading club with the intention and aim of turning "pro." This book is designed to furnish all of them with an equally sound orientation and a solid foundation for successful training.

There is important information in these pages for parents, brothers and sisters, grandparents and friends, too. Together with your child, you will use this book as a training companion, workbook and reference book all in one. Your help will no doubt also be needed at other times, for instance in

setting up performance charts or with the personal journal entries. Rejoice in your little soccer enthusiast's goals and victories. Children crave our approval, praise and recognition. Commiserate with them when things do not pan out. Not everybody has the stuff of world-class soccer players.

Above all, playing soccer is fun, it fosters social contacts, develops ambition as well as the ability to assert oneself. By training together and playing matches as a team, children and teenagers learn how to transcend themselves and how to handle success as well as failure. Character traits like fairness, reliability, punctuality, order, perseverance, willingness to take risks, courage and team spirit are cultivated and refined and will also be of great use in all other areas of your child's life.

Dear Coach!

Good youth training is based on the complete and well-rounded development of your charges' personalities. It can be viewed as a learning process because it advocates control and self-control. It is a socializing instrument because training, especially as a group, drills social norms, rules and behavioral patterns. Training children and teenagers is a rich experience, taking moods, feelings and emotions into account.

It promises positive experiences, matures evolving wants and desires, transpires in a warm, loving and open environment. Your young soccer players are your partners in this adventure – provided they are actively included in the training process and are given sufficient freedom to have a say in matters. Thus, do not regard your young kickers as mere recipients of your instructions but rather as partners in a mutual training adventure. Tell them why and when it is necessary for them to do whichever exercise, plus what degree of exertion is especially beneficial for each respective part of their training.

It is our desire to give the children a workbook to accompany their training. They can read about various things they have learned as well as record their aims, objectives and motivation and track their personal performance. Of course no book can replace the experiences gained from years of training. And the opinions of coaches, sports scientists and "book writers" will sometimes be at odds, too. Consider this soccer book as a supplement to your training program and as an aid in approaching the sport from a perspective outside your shared training.

A good youth coach is continually thinking not only about how he or she can instill technique or develop physical fitness during soccer training sessions, but also how he or she can actively involve the kids in the drilling and training process, so as to qualitatively enhance the sessions as well as consciously support the overall personal development of his or her players.

We wish you continued fun and success with your up-and-coming young kickers!

..........PHOTO AND ILLUSTRATION CREDITS

Cover photo: Asa photo agency

Drawings: Katrin Barth
Photos::   Michael Ballack, Kerstin Dischereit, TV Rheinbeck, Erich
               Rutemöller, Gerd Schumacher, Regina Weitz

Cover design: Birgit Engelen

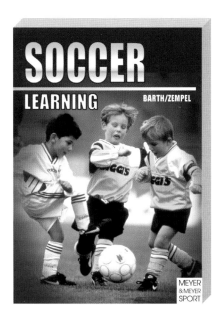

Barth/Zempel
Learning ... Soccer

Soccer is "in", and even the youngest children don't just want to kick the ball around, they want to know everything about their favorite sport. Billy "the magic mouse", accompanies children through the book, and talks about all you need to know about soccer. It answers questions on soccer gear, regulations, soccer clubs, the history of soccer, and everything else children are interested in, to become a celebrated "magic mouse" some day. Basic techniques are explained so they are easily understood, and suggestions are made to promote independent practice. Billy's quizzes and puzzles, as well as opportunities for filling out and coloring in, quickly make this book a constant companion for young soccer players.

136 pages, full-colour print
several photos, numerous drawings
Paperback, 5 $^{3}/_{4}$" x 8 $^{1}/_{4}$"
ISBN: 1-84126-130-0
£ 9.95 UK / $ 14.95 US
$ 20.95 CDN / € 14.90

MEYER & MEYER Sport | sales@m-m-sports.com | www.m-m-sports.com

MEYER
& MEYER
SPORT

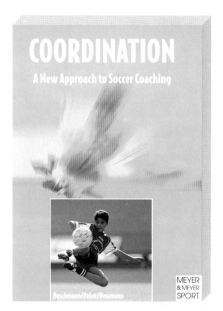

Jürgen Buschmann/
Klaus Pabst/Hubertus Bussmann
Coordination
**A New Approach
to Soccer Coaching**

Modern soccer is distinguished by perfect ball and
body control at top speed. For this reason training in
movement and ball skills are becoming more and
more important. Coordination skills are therefore
among those factors that determine performance in
soccer. This book describes numerous coordinative
forms of play and training and is for all coaches and
sports teachers in schools and clubs.

120 pages
Two-colour print
52 photos, 85 figures
Paperback, $5^3/4''$ x $8^1/4''$
ISBN 1-84126-063-0
£ 9.95 UK / $ 14.95 US
$ 20.95 CDN / € 14.90

Anz training soccer 8/03

MEYER & MEYER Sport | sales@m-m-sports.com | www.m-m-sports.com